解析亨利·基辛格
《世界秩序》

AN ANALYSIS OF
HENRY KISSINGER'S
WORLD ORDER:
Reflections on the Character of Nations and the Course of History

Bryan R. Gibson ◎ 著

于金权 ◎ 译

上海外语教育出版社
SHANGHAI FOREIGN LANGUAGE EDUCATION PRESS

目　录

引言 ··· 1
   亨利·基辛格其人 2
   《世界秩序》的主要内容 3
   《世界秩序》的学术价值 5

第一部分：学术渊源 ··· 9
   1. 作者生平与历史背景 10
   2. 学术背景 15
   3. 主导命题 19
   4. 作者贡献 24

第二部分：学术思想 ··· 29
   5. 思想主脉 30
   6. 思想支脉 35
   7. 历史成就 39
   8. 著作地位 43

第三部分：学术影响 ··· 47
   9. 最初反响 48
   10. 后续争议 52
   11. 当代印迹 56
   12. 未来展望 60

术语表 ·· 63
人名表 ·· 71

CONTENTS

WAYS IN TO THE TEXT	79
Who Is Henry Kissinger?	80
What Does *World Order* Say?	81
Why Does *World Order* Matter?	84
SECTION 1: INFLUENCES	87
Module 1: The Author and the Historical Context	88
Module 2: Academic Context	93
Module 3: The Problem	98
Module 4: The Author's Contribution	104
SECTION 2: IDEAS	109
Module 5: Main Ideas	110
Module 6: Secondary Ideas	116
Module 7: Achievement	121
Module 8: Place in the Author's Work	126
SECTION 3: IMPACT	131
Module 9: The First Responses	132
Module 10: The Evolving Debate	137
Module 11: Impact and Influence Today	142
Module 12: Where Next?	147
Glossary of Terms	151
People Mentioned in the Text	161
Works Cited	166

引言

要 点

- 亨利·基辛格(1923 年生)是一位德裔美国学者、外交家和荣获诺贝尔和平奖*的政治家。

- 他的著作《世界秩序》(2014)从历史的角度论述了世界各地如何理解他所称的"世界秩序"*——一个国际关系的稳定体系。

- 该书考察了 1991 年苏联解体后"现实主义者"*与"自由国际主义者"*之间不断升级的无休止争论。现实主义者认为不稳定和冲突的风险依然居高不下,而自由国际主义者坚信,如果采取措施以推进有利于自由世界秩序的国际结构,国家间的合作将增加。

亨利·基辛格其人

海因茨·阿尔弗雷德·"亨利"·基辛格是 20 世纪最负盛名又最具争议的政治家之一。他在理查德·尼克松*和杰拉尔德·福特*执政期间曾担任美国国家安全顾问*(1969—1975)和国务卿*(1973—1977)。[1] 在此期间,他曾受到指控涉嫌侵犯人权。

基辛格于 1923 年出生于德国南部巴伐利亚州的富尔特镇。[2] 他所在的犹太家族十分兴旺庞大。随着 1933 年纳粹党的上台,德国的犹太人受到了纳粹主义的迫害,他的家族受到的威胁日益加重。1938 年,与许多德国犹太人一样,基辛格一家人也逃往了美国。到美国后,基辛格将其名英文化为"亨利",不过他的英语依然有很重的德国口音。1941 年,美国参加第二次世界大战*后,基辛格应征入伍,正式成为美国公民。他流利的德语和关于纳粹德国*的知识促使他从事反间谍工作（防止间谍活动），在这方面，他表现出众。

战后，基辛格被哈佛大学录取，学习政治学和哲学。他于1950年、1951年和1954年分别获得了文学学士学位、文学硕士学位和哲学博士学位。基辛格在哈佛大学获得了教职，成为直言批评美国外交政策的学者。这引起了右翼共和党*高层（比如总统候选人纳尔逊·洛克菲勒*）对他的关注。1969年，理查德·尼克松总统邀请基辛格担任其安全顾问；随后五年，他们一起致力于重塑国际政治版图。

基辛格拥有高超的外交技能，促使美国于1973年撤出越南战争*，因而获得了诺贝尔和平奖。越南战争是冷战*时期一场残酷的代理人战争（即两个超级大国引发了战争，但没有实际参与冲突），战争双方是美国支持的南越和苏联、中国支持的北越。1977年离开公职后，基辛格依旧为美国政府提供外交政策咨询。

《世界秩序》的主要内容

《世界秩序：反思国家特征和历史进程》提供的历史分析是针对人类面临的一个极具挑战性的问题：什么是世界秩序——大体而言，即一个国际关系的稳定体系——以及我们该如何促成一种普世接受的国际体系形式？

为了回答这个问题，基辛格分析了四种主要的世界秩序形式：

- 欧洲的"威斯特伐利亚"体系*。这一体系建立在主权*（统治特定领土的权利）、合法性*（合乎法律）、均势*（国家间军事和政治力量的平衡，构成了国际秩序）、国家利益*（对一个国家而言，对其政治、军事、经济或外交名声和舒适度或其生存至关重要的东西）的观念之上。
- 普世的伊斯兰秩序*（这一秩序建立在伊斯兰信仰至高无上的观念之上）。
- "以中国为中心"*的中国秩序（按照这个秩序，中国位于文明世界的中心）。
- 美国秩序，基于自由、公正和代议制民主的观念。

他还阐述了日本、印度和波斯（现代的伊朗）形成的三种次级的世界秩序观。基辛格指出，日本和印度各自形成了不同于中国秩序的世界秩序观，主要是因为它们在地理上与中国互相隔离——日本是一个岛国，而印度和中国之间隔着喜马拉雅山脉。与此类似，波斯独自形成了世界秩序，这是因为其所处的地理位置就在多个文明的交汇处：亚洲、欧洲、印度和伊斯兰。虽然波斯把伊斯兰教奉为国教，但其古代遗产和信奉伊斯兰少数派什叶派*教义的决定使它形成了与众不同的世界秩序观。

如今，占主导地位的世界秩序观是残酷的三十年战争*之后形成于17世纪的威斯特伐利亚体系。（三十年战争是一个被称为神圣罗马帝国*的政治实体与几个日尔曼国家之间的一场冲突，随后不断升级，大部分欧洲国家都卷入其中。）战争接近尾声的时候，欧洲大陆的大部分国家都在遭受这场重大冲突带来的后果，于是欧洲政治家推演出主权、合法性、均势和国家利益的观念，希望以此来解决今后出现的分歧。1648年，签署威斯特伐利亚和约*（该和约结束了三十年战争）时，各签约国一致同意尊重各国领导人的合法性，不干涉其内政。他们互设外交事务代表办事处，和平解决争端。更为重要的是，各签约国原则上一致同意，要是一国变得过于强大，其他国家将结成联盟，重建体系的平衡，这就是后来为人熟知的"均势"。

经过几百年的演变和不可避免的改进,威斯特伐利亚体系大体而言依然维系着现代国际关系。然而,正如基辛格在《世界秩序》中所示,它不再普遍适用,不再被人轻易接受;当前的国际体系可以理解为殖民*时代的遗物——即欧洲"主人"强加给殖民对象的一种体系。现今,其正面临着诸如中国、伊斯兰以及美国的世界秩序概念发起的挑战。

比如,中国体系以中国为中心,将中国视为世界的中心和新兴的超级大国,今后中国势必希望在更广泛的世界不断施加它的影响。根据普世的伊斯兰世界秩序观,那些信奉伊斯兰教的人属于达尔·阿勒·伊斯兰*——即"伊斯兰之家"——的一部分,而那些不信奉伊斯兰教的人属于达尔·阿勒·哈珀*,意为"征伐之地",被视为外人,即"他者",他们要么皈依,要么面临真主的愤怒。伊拉克和大叙利亚伊斯兰国(ISIS)*、其盟友基地组织*及其在尼日利亚的分支博科圣地等武装团体*就宣扬这一观念的最极端形式。

《世界秩序》的学术价值

当前,研究美国外交政策和国际关系的学者就如何构建一种新的世界秩序争论不休,《世界秩序》对这场争论作出了巨大贡献。这场争论在很大程度上是冷战(1947—1991)结束的产物。冷战不但造成了军事威胁,还是第二次世界大战两个最显著的受益者美国和苏联之间在意识形态上的对峙。1945年后,这两个国家都成为超级大国*,但在意识形态上却完全对立。

两国均想把自己的意识形态强加给世界。苏联是一个社会主义大国（即财产归公共所有，劳动致力于公共利益）。美国自认为是"自由世界"（指世界上非社会主义的国家）的领导者，代表资本主义*（一种产业和贸易归私人所有的经济制度）和民主。1991年，苏联解体，美国价值观似乎占了上风。然而，冷战给东方集团*带来了一定程度上的稳定；1991年后，不可回避的问题是，有什么体系（如果存在的话）可以加以替代。

当时，美国成为唯一的超级大国。在美国，学者可分为两大派。"现实主义者"，比如国际关系学者约翰·米尔斯海默*和斯蒂芬·沃尔特*，认为苏联解体几乎不会影响国际秩序，因为国际政治的本质没有发生根本性的变化：各国将继续依照"如何最好地行使自己的权力"这一原则运行，从自己的国家利益出发评估和应对事件。按照这种分析，国家间发生冲突的几率不太可能减少。

第二个派别，"自由国际主义者"，比如国际关系学者安妮-玛丽·斯劳特*、罗伯特·基欧汉*和小约瑟夫·奈*，认为后冷战时代将迎来国际合作新时代，大国（英国、法国、德国、俄罗斯、中国和美国）的权力政治将成为历史。这一派更加乐观，认为如果联合国*等国际组织能够得到加强，国家间的冲突将减少。这种观点并不反对军事干预，比如在政府无力或不愿意保护其公民的情况下进行干预。

尽管基辛格自称现实主义者，但《世界秩序》中的观点表明他往往介于这两派中间。一方面，他偏现实主义的观点体现在，他认为施行权力（力量投射）和获取合法性——大体而言，合法性是一个实体存在的法律基础——对于外交关系的实施至关重要，是否采取外交干预必须基于一个国家的国家利益而非理论上的道德观。另一方面，他也持有自由派的立场，认为需要加强国际机构，以促进合作，防止冲突。

---

1. 克里斯托弗·希钦斯：《审判基辛格》，伦敦：沃索出版社，2001年。
2. 罗伯特·达莱克：《尼克松与基辛格：权力伙伴》，伦敦：哈珀柯林斯出版社，2007年，第34页。

第一部分：学术渊源

1 作者生平与历史背景

要点 🗝

- 《世界秩序》对于如何构建新世界秩序的长期争论作出了重大贡献。

- 亨利·基辛格是荣获诺贝尔奖*的外交家、学者以及具有国际声望的政治家。1973年至1977年,他担任美国的国务卿*——美国政府中最高的外交职位。

- 冷战是以苏联和美国为首的两大阵营之间长达数十年的核僵局,随着1991年苏联解体而终结。冷战结束后,一个稳定的世界秩序迟迟无法建立,这让基辛格坚信必须撰写这本书。

为何要读这部著作?

如何构建一种普世接受的世界秩序——各国公民一致认同的国际关系、均势和治理的一种结构?这是人类面临的最大挑战之一,而亨利·基辛格的《世界秩序:反思国家特征和历史进程》对此提供了重要分析。作为西方世界最受尊重的政治家和外交政策分析师之一,基辛格具有得天独厚的条件探讨这个核心问题。他表明当前存在四种主要的世界秩序观:

- 欧洲的威斯特伐利亚体系
- 普世的伊斯兰秩序
- 中国的以中国为中心的秩序
- 美国秩序

在这些世界秩序观中,当前占主导地位的体系是始于17世纪、随后频繁剧变的威斯特伐利亚体系，这一秩序建立在主权、合法性、均势和国家利益的观念之上。然而，正如基辛格在《世界秩序》中直言不讳地指出，这是一个在各个方面都遭到攻击的体系。构建可行的新世界秩序之路依然不明朗。

在那些对世界秩序观或者更宽泛意义上的国际政治感兴趣的人看来，《世界秩序》全面梳理了世界历史，对历史上的重大冲突或稳定状态的关键成因见解独到。这在当今显得尤为重要，因为各国在 20 世纪面临的典型挑战——不仅仅是战争，还有冷战——已经发生了重大变化。新的威胁并非来自传统意义上的国家实体，最明显的例子就是被称为伊拉克和大叙利亚伊斯兰国（ISIS）的武装宗教团体。同样，大自然也以极具破坏性的流行疾病展现其威胁，比如 2014 年爆发的埃博拉病毒传染病导致西非近 2.5 万人丧生。[1] 由于各国面临的挑战日益全球化，构建一种新的世界秩序更加迫在眉睫。[2]

> "如果我必须在公正但无序和不公正但有序之间选择的话，我总是会选择后者。"
> —— 亨利·基辛格，引自罗伯特·达莱克《尼克松与基辛格》

作者生平

海因茨·阿尔弗雷德·基辛格 1923 年 5 月 27 日出生于巴伐利亚州富尔特镇，该小镇位于遭受第一次世界大战*重创后建立起来的脆弱的德意志联邦共和国魏玛*境内。他出身于一个中产阶级犹太家庭。他的母亲保拉·斯特恩来自一个富裕的家庭，他的父亲路易斯是一所公立学校的校长。基辛格家族在镇上相当有名望。海因

茨·基辛格还有一个弟弟叫瓦特。³

青少年时期的基辛格一年比一年过得艰难。对于一个充满求知欲的犹太男孩而言，1933年阿道夫·希特勒*及其领导的纳粹党上台使德国变成了一个极不友好且相当危险的地方。⁴1938年8月，海因茨·基辛格及其家人从德国逃到了亲戚所在的美国。尽管他把自己的德国名字"海因茨"改成了"亨利"，他的德国口音依然很明显。

1943年，基辛格入伍参加了第二次世界大战。他先被派往法国，随后是德国；1945年战争结束后，他在德国的去纳粹化过程中发挥了积极作用。在那里，他找到了自己的第一份职业。他的才智、流利的德语以及在纳粹德国的亲身经历让他脱颖而出。

战后，基辛格进入哈佛大学深造，每天学习16个小时，获得了最高荣誉。1949年，正是在哈佛大学，他与安·弗莱彻结为夫妇。他们育有两个孩子，1964年以离婚告终。获得文学学士学位后，基辛格继续深造，分别于1951年和1954年获得了文学硕士学位和哲学博士学位。

在哈佛大学获得终身教职后，基辛格发表了一系列言辞犀利的文章，猛烈抨击美国的外交政策，这引起了当时的总统候选人、商人纳尔逊·洛克菲勒的注意，后者将基辛格聘为竞选顾问。1968年大选，洛克菲勒竞选共和党*总统候选人落败后，获得提名（并赢得大选）的理查德·尼克松*聘请基辛格担任国家安全顾问*。1973年，尼克松任命他为国务卿。1977年离开公职后，基辛格依然是"如何实施美国外交政策"这一辩论中的核心人物。

创作背景

冷战对基辛格的学术生涯产生了深远的影响。正当他在哈佛大学开始求学之际,这场美国和苏联之间的意识形态和地缘战略*冲突拉开了帷幕。(在地缘战略冲突中,政治和国际关系受到地理环境和军事、政治战略的影响。)基辛格的博士论文《和平、合法性和均势:论卡斯尔雷*和梅特涅*的政治才能》以史为鉴,主要论述了政治家在维也纳会议*中发挥的作用,该会议在1815年拿破仑·波拿巴*战败后促成了一种欧洲新秩序。

1955年至1961年间,基辛格发表了许多文章,批评外交政策制定的传统观念,使他成为首屈一指的外交政策评论家,获得了全国关注。1955年,他在《外交》杂志上发文抨击艾森豪威尔*总统当局为了避免与苏联开战而推行大规模核报复——即确保互相毁灭*——的政策,并提议采用打有限战争*的策略来应对苏联影响力的扩张。1957年,当这篇文章以《核武器与外交政策》为题成书出版后,旋即成为畅销书,基辛格成了家喻户晓的人物。

如今,基辛格因其在尼克松总统(他因深陷一场政治丑闻,丢尽脸面而被迫辞职)及其继任者杰拉尔德·福特*两届政府担任要职而闻名于世。在这期间,基辛格将自己有关外交政策的知识付诸实践,在外交政策方面取得了一系列无与伦比的成功。在1972年至1973年间的18个月内,基辛格协助"结束了越南战争,对中国打开了大门;为抵抗北越攻势而不断升级军事措施的同时与苏联举行了峰会,让苏联盟国埃及转而与美国紧密合作;在中东促成了两份撤军协议……启动了欧洲安全会议,从长期的结果来看,欧安会严重削弱了苏联对东欧的控制。"[5]

1. 美国疾病防控中心:"2014年西非埃博拉病毒爆发——病例数量统计",登录日期2015年11月18日,https://www.cdc.gov/vhf/ebola/outbreaks/2014-west-africa/case-counts.html。
2. 沃尔夫冈·伊申格尔:"基辛格的世界:如何维护全球秩序",《外交》,2015年3/4月,登录日期2015年10月1日,https://www.foreignaffairs.com/reviews/2015-03-01/world-according-kissinger。
3. 罗伯特·达莱克:《尼克松与基辛格》,伦敦:哈珀柯林斯出版社,2007年,第34页。
4. 达莱克:《尼克松与基辛格》,第34页。
5. 亨利·基辛格:《世界秩序》,纽约:企鹅出版社,2015年,第307—308页。

2 学术背景

要点

- 《世界秩序》与两大研究领域密切相关：外交历史学和国际关系学。前者关注外交关系的历史，而后者关注国家及非政府组织之间的关系。

- 国际关系学理论分为两个阵营：现实主义者和自由国际主义者。现实主义者认为，当国家利益受到威胁时，各国就会诉诸武力，冲突是国际政治的常态。自由国际主义者认为，如果没有占主导地位的强国（又称为霸权国家*），各国往往就会合作，这种合作是国际政治的准则。

- 亨利·基辛格是一位现实主义者，这一点从他在白宫任职期间处理外交关系的方式中显露无遗。

著作语境

亨利·基辛格的《世界秩序：反思国家特征和历史进程》适用于两个紧密相连的学科：外交历史学和国际关系学。尽管基辛格是著名的外交政策实践者，但实际上他的本职是一位外交历史学家，其研究主要关注外交关系的实施。

外交历史学家利用档案研究、回忆录、口述历史和文献分析等手段来形成对国家间关系的历史性认识。如今，随着研究者可以从政府获得越来越多的文件，这一领域作为一个学科越来越受欢迎；在商业方面亦是如此，大型出版社出版的有关外交的著作都大获成功。基辛格的《世界秩序》就是一个典型的例子。

国际关系学更像是政治学的一个子学科，主要关注国家及非政府机构间如何互动。非政府机构包括世界银行*（成立该组织旨在给发展中国家提供贷款以促进经济改革）这样的国际组织、企业（比如微软公司、苹果公司和 Gap 公司）或者恐怖组织（当前广为人知的例子就是伊拉克和大叙利亚伊斯兰国）。

这绝不是一个全新的领域。历代学者和哲学家，其中包括古希腊哲学家亚里士多德*、古希腊历史学家修昔底德*和 15—16 世纪的政治理论家尼科洛·马基雅维利*，早就对各民族（或国家）之间如何互动产生了兴趣并且形成了完备的理论，以期对其作出解释。这些理论，比如现实主义或者理想主义*，会对外交政策实践者如何操作以及做决策时考虑哪些因素产生重大影响。

> "我想让你见见亨利·基辛格，他是伊曼努尔·康德和巴鲁赫·德·斯宾诺莎的结合体。"
> ——威廉·扬德尔·埃利奥特，引自罗伯特·达莱克
> 《尼克松与基辛格》

学科概览

作为一部外交历史学著作，基辛格的《世界秩序》继承了 19 世纪德国历史学家、被誉为外交历史学之父的利奥波德·冯·兰克*的学术遗产。兰克认为，唯有通过档案研究和历史文献分析，才能获得所有客观事实——对历史事件的准确描述。在兰克看来，按时间顺序梳理历史事件最有助于理解历史事件，这也是呈现因果关系的最佳方式。这两种技巧在《世界秩序》以及基辛格以前的历史著作和回忆录中都显而易见，他经常利用这两种技巧处理其在白宫任

职期间的文件。

基辛格的著作也参与了国际关系学者之间的重要争论。这些学者根据历史渊源可以分为两大学派：现实主义者和理想主义者。现实主义者，比如基辛格、西奥多·罗斯福*和理查德·尼克松，把国际政治视为主权国家（主权国家是一个自治的独立国家）互相制衡权力*的问题。这三个人还坚信美国力量的辐射力。正如国际关系学者小约瑟夫·奈指出，对于现实主义者而言，"世界秩序是大国之间权力稳定分配的产物。"[1] 基辛格与现实主义的渊源可以回溯到哈佛大学求学时期，汉斯·摩根索*——哈佛大学的一位古典现实主义者*——让他坚信全球政治由国家力量和对国家利益的冷静盘算界定。[2]

另一个是理想主义（或者说自由主义）学派。就美国而言，主要拥护者为伍德罗·威尔逊*总统（1913年至1921年期间担任美国总统）和吉米·卡特*总统（执政时间为1977年至1981年）。理想主义将其分析建立在国家和人民本性善良的假设之上，倡导民主和人权等价值观。理想主义者认为，应该推进国家间的合作，尤其通过联合国*等国际组织来推进合作。

学术渊源

在基辛格还是一名年轻学者的时候，两个人对他的学术发展和后来的事业产生了直接影响。第一位是弗里茨·克雷默*，同样是一名流亡美国的德国学者，基辛格加入美国军队后遇到了他。据基辛格的传记作家记载，"克雷默帮忙给亨利安排了工作，增强了他的自信心，并让他日益觉得他不仅仅是一个归化美国人，还是一个德国人……一个对国际事务抱有强烈兴趣的欧洲人。"[3] 更为重要的是，正是克雷默说服基辛格利用《退伍军人权利法案》*（该法案旨在为退役军人提供福利）进入哈佛大学学习并申请纽约的州立奖学金。⁴

在哈佛大学，基辛格遇到了第二位对他产生重大影响的人：历史学家威廉·扬德尔·埃利奥特*。他是政府治理方面的著名学者，曾担任六位美国总统的总统顾问，还欣然同意成为基辛格的导师。埃利奥特激发了基辛格的求知欲，比如，要求他阅读25部伊曼努尔·康德的著作并撰写书评。为了打动导师，基辛格在短短三个月内完成了这份作业，促使埃利奥特在其同事面前这样描述，"过去5年所带的学生中，没有人像基辛格先生一样展现出这样的深度和哲学洞见"；他还把基辛格视为"康德和（荷兰著名哲学家）斯宾诺莎的结合体"。⁵ 通过埃利奥特的鼓励、指导和支持，基辛格申请了哈佛大学的博士课程并被录取。

---

1. 小约瑟夫·奈：''什么样的新世界秩序？''，《外交》，1992年春，第84—85页，登录日期2015年12月7日，https://www.foreignaffairs.com/articles/1992-03-01/what-new-world-order。
2. 汉斯·摩根索：《国家间政治：权力斗争与和平》，纽约：科诺夫出版社，1948年。
3. 罗伯特·达莱克：《尼克松与基辛格》，伦敦：哈珀柯林斯出版社，2007年，第34—38页。
4. 达莱克：《尼克松与基辛格》，第39页。
5. 达莱克：《尼克松与基辛格》，第41页。

3. 主导命题

要点

- 2014年《世界秩序》出版的时候，关于世界秩序本质的争论在20世纪90年代和21世纪伊始的阶段性活跃之后渐趋平息。
- 在20世纪90年代，国际关系的现实主义学派认为，新世界秩序将基于西方个人主义与自由价值观的辐射，世界主要文明的断层带间，混乱或将持续存在。国际关系的自由主义学派认为，通过加强和改革联合国等国际机构可以构建新世界秩序。
- 《世界秩序》介于两者之间，融合了现实主义者和自由主义者的观点。

核心问题

亨利·基辛格《世界秩序》讨论的核心问题是：什么是世界秩序？全世界如何看待世界秩序？新世界秩序的理念并不是特别新颖，也不是基辛格著作的独特之处，这直接反映了冷战结束以来国际关系学者间的争论（特别是有关美国外交政策的问题）。1991年苏联解体、东欧剧变后，新世界秩序这个术语与乔治·赫伯特·沃克·布什*总统的政府紧密相连。布什政府宣布其有意放弃冷战时代的单边主义*（一个单一的国家未获得其他国家的同意或支持就采取行动），支持多边*外交，但不排除使用武力。

将东西德国分隔开的柏林墙*倒塌后，美国政治学家弗朗西斯·福山*1989年发表的《历史的终结？》一文引发了"冷战后的世界秩序会怎么样"的激烈争论，这篇文章后来发展成于 1992 年出版的著作《历史的终结与最后的人》。福山认为，新的世界秩序将建立在西方的自由和民主传统之上。在随后的 25 年间，众多国际关系的学者参与了这场争论。尽管如此，冷战后的秩序会是什么样子以及美国在塑造这一秩序中会发挥什么作用的问题依然没有达成共识。

> "本书源自与查理·希尔在一次晚宴上的谈话……恍如隔世，彼时我担任国务卿的时候，他是（国务院）政策规划司的重要成员……在那次晚宴上，我们共同得出结论：世界秩序观的危机是我们当下面临的最根本的国际问题。"
>
> —— 亨利·基辛格：《世界秩序：反思国家特征和历史进程》

参与者

福山的《历史的终结与最后的人》出版后，多名学者就"冷战后的世界秩序会怎么样"的问题提出了针锋相对的观点。1992 年，国际关系学者小约瑟夫·奈在《外交》杂志上发表了一篇文章回应福山，问道："什么样的新世界秩序？"在他看来，"历史并没有终结，冷战后的世界正在见证各种国际冲突根源的历史回归。"[1] 翌年，美国政治学家塞缪尔·菲利普斯·亨廷顿*在《文明的冲突？》一文及随后的著作《文明的冲突与世界秩序的重建》（1996）中回应了福山。亨廷顿认为，"在新兴的（冷战后）世界，西方信奉的西方文化普世性遇到了三个问题：它是错误的；它是不道德的；它是危险的。"[2] 在亨廷顿看来，"这个新世界中冲突的根源不会是意识形态或经济上的。人类的巨大分歧和冲突的主要来源将是

文化上的。国家将依然是处理世界事务的最强大角色，但是全球政治的冲突将发生在不同文明的国家和群体之间。"³

当时的论战

福山和亨廷顿的观点激起了自由主义国际关系学者的回应，他们认为公正的新世界秩序依赖于国际机构的加强。1997年，国际关系学者安妮-玛丽·斯劳特发表了《真正的新世界秩序》一文，她在文中指出一种新的世界秩序正在出现，但并不是以基辛格所认为的超国家（凌驾于国家之上）的机构形式，比如联合国或者世界银行。相反，斯劳特认为这种新的世界秩序实际上正在从亚国家（国家之下的）层面出现，在这个层面上，法院、监管机构以及世界自然基金会*和绿色和平组织*等非政府组织或机构的代表组成的网络错综复杂、互相联系，他们通力合作应对犯罪、恐怖主义、环境恶化和国际关系等跨国问题——她把这一过程称为"跨政府主义"。⁴ 革命性的技术发展，最重要的是互联网的发展，推动了这个过程。

2001年，国际关系教授约翰·米尔斯海默*借助其著作《大国政治的悲剧》参与了关于后冷战世界的辩论。在书中，米尔斯海默提出了进攻性现实主义*的概念。这种概念认为国际体系处于无政府状态（即不受统治）、大国是全球政治的主要参与者、所有国家都拥有进攻的能力、各国永远无法确定彼此的意图、生存是最主要目标以及所有国家都是理性的参与者（即它们根据理性的决定采取行动）。简言之，米尔斯海默认为，冷战的终结并不会减少最强大国家间持续竞争的可能性。⁵

2001年9月11日恐怖袭击（911事件）*及随之而来的反恐战争*——即美国主导的在整个中东针对非政府组织展开的行动和美

国主导的阿富汗*战争与伊拉克*战争——之后，有关新世界秩序的辩论不知何去何从。然而，在21世纪头十年中期，学界强烈反对乔治·W.布什政府的单边主义（即倾向于采取单独行动），反对其努力借助美国在国际组织中的主导地位来推行其短视的"美国主导的世界秩序"。[6]发动失败的伊拉克战争的两位核心人物约翰·博尔顿*和保罗·沃尔福威茨*分别被任命为美国驻联合国大使和世界银行总裁，自由派人士对此特别失望。

作为回应，保罗·肯尼迪*在其著作《人类议会：联合国的过去、现在与未来》（2006）中呼吁加强国际组织（尤其是联合国）的力量。与此类似，2009年，政府学学者斯蒂芬·布鲁克斯*和威廉·沃尔福思*认为，贝拉克·奥巴马*总统的新政府要采取五个步骤来改革国际机构、推行新秩序：

- 强调倡导的改革互利共赢；
- 确保修订后的框架能够给公众带来福利，比如遏制恐怖主义、稳定全球经济；
- 将倡导的秩序与现行秩序联系起来；
- 考虑其他国家可能的反对并采取行动减少它们的法律效力；
- 说服他国改变势在必行。[7]

---

1. 小约瑟夫·奈："什么样的新世界秩序？"，《外交》，1992年春，第84—85页，登录日期2015年12月7日，https://www.foreignaffairs.com/articles/1992-03-01/what-new-world-order。

2. 塞缪尔·菲利普斯·亨廷顿：《文明的冲突与世界秩序的重建》，伦敦：西蒙与舒斯特出版社，2002 年，第 310 页。
3. 塞缪尔·菲利普斯·亨廷顿："文明的冲突？"，《外交》，1993 年夏，第 22 页，登录日期 2015 年 12 月 7 日，https://www.foreignaffairs.com/articles/united-states/1993-06-01/clash-civilizations。
4. 安妮－玛丽·斯劳特："真正的新世界秩序"，《外交》，1997 年 9/10 月，第 183—184 页，登录日期 2015 年 12 月 7 日，https://www.foreignaffairs.com/articles/1997-09-01/real-new-world-order。
5. 约翰·J. 米尔斯海默：《大国政治的悲剧》，纽约：W.W. 诺顿出版社，2001 年。
6. 丹尼尔·W. 德雷兹纳："新之又新的世界秩序"，《外交》，2007 年 3/4 月，第 34—46 页，登录日期 2015 年 12 月 7 日，https://www.foreignaffairs.com/articles/2007-03-01/new-new-world-order。
7. 斯蒂芬·G. 布鲁克斯和威廉·C. 沃尔福思："重塑世界秩序"，《外交》，2009 年 3/4 月，第 59 页，登录日期 2015 年 12 月 7 日，https://www.foreignaffairs.com/articles/2009-03-01/reshaping-world-order。

4 作者贡献

要点

- 亨利·基辛格并没有具体阐述如何构建新世界秩序。
- 他考察了全球不同地区对于世界秩序的不同理解以及这些理解是如何随着时间的推移而发生演变的。
- 以当前国际关系现实主义者和自由主义者之间的辩论为依托,基辛格基于欧洲、伊斯兰、亚洲和美国的历史阐明了这些文明是如何理解世界秩序的概念的。

作者目标

撰写《世界秩序》时,亨利·基辛格的主要目标是阐释世界秩序概念的各种解读,说明这些解读的形成渊源并指出未来构建普世世界秩序可能遇到的障碍。对他而言,核心问题是"从来不曾存在一个真正全球性的'世界秩序'";[1] 直到近期,世界各地区之间至多只存在有限的沟通。因此,不同地区、不同文明对世界秩序产生了不同观点:欧洲的威斯特伐利亚秩序,以主权和合法性为原则;伊斯兰秩序,以穆斯林信仰至高无上的观念为基础;以中国为中心的亚洲秩序,按照这种秩序,中国应该自动被认为是任何世界秩序的中心;美国秩序,深受民主和自由原则影响;以及两种次级亚洲秩序——日本秩序和印度秩序,因与中国在地理位置上相对独立而形成。

然而,以前互相隔离的文明现在能够即时沟通,这对基辛格来说是一件喜忧参半的事情。一方面,这些全球性的互动能够让新理念广泛传播，最终形成基辛格梦寐以求的普遍秩序的基础。另一方面，其中有些理念——尤其是中国和伊斯兰的理念——本身与西方主流的世界秩序愿景是对立的。

虽然基辛格指出了这些对世界秩序的不同解读，但他并没有提出可能解决当前僵局的办法。

> "我们的时代锲而不舍地，有时几乎是不顾一切地追求一个世界秩序的概念。世界混乱无序，各国之间却又史无前例地相互依存，从而构成了种种威胁：大规模杀伤性武器在扩散，国家解体，环境恶化，种族灭绝现象层出不穷，有可能将冲突推向人类无法控制或无法想象地步的新技术正在发展。"
>
> ——亨利·基辛格：《世界秩序：反思国家特征和历史进程》

研究方法

为了实现其目标，基辛格采用了按地区展开历史分析的方法。他首先考察了欧洲的历史，具体而言，考察了威斯特伐利亚和约——这一系列和约于1648年结束了被称为"神圣罗马帝国"的政治实体和其他几个欧洲邻国之间的三十年战争——如何促进发展了主权、均势和合法性等现代概念。欧洲殖民大国——英国、法国、葡萄牙和西班牙等国——随后在其殖民帝国（即他们在海外掠夺、统治和剥削的领土）中采用了这些理念。因此，全球主流的世界秩序观就基于这些威斯特伐利亚概念之上，在国际组织（比如联合国）中备受尊崇。

然而，单单一种西方的世界秩序观在世界各地盛行，并不意味着它是被普遍接受的。因而，基辛格紧接着考察了伊斯兰、亚洲（即日本和印度）、中国和美国的世界秩序观，它们与欧洲形成的世界秩序观在很多方面都有差异。在考察每一种世界秩序观时，基辛格通过历史分析阐明了这些概念的形成渊源：通常是基于每个地区的历史经历和与具有威胁性的欧洲强国的互动。即使是美国的世界秩序观，虽然从技术上来说继承了威斯特伐利亚秩序，但与其欧洲的姊妹概念也有差异，因为美国的世界秩序观以自由、公正和民主为前提。阿道夫·希特勒*或者约瑟夫·斯大林*——两位均为欧洲领导人，代表政治派别的极端——几乎不可能接受这些概念的合法性，即使他们会在不同程度上接受威斯特伐利亚秩序的核心概念。

时代贡献

《世界秩序》写于基辛格璀璨的学术和政治生涯将近尾声之际——牢记这一点至关重要。作为一名学者，基辛格的著作持续不断地关注与世界秩序有关的问题。比如，《世界秩序》的头两章探讨了威斯特伐利亚秩序的建立和维也纳会议。维也纳会议于1815年召开，决定了拿破仑·波拿巴（这位法国皇帝曾将欧洲大陆大部分地区都纳入法国统治之下）战败后新的欧洲政治秩序。关于这两个话题的讨论在基辛格的大部分著作中都出现过。事实上，这两个话题构成了基辛格前期学术著作《重建的世界：梅特涅、卡斯尔雷与和平问题，1812—1822》（1957）的基础，该著分析了外交家在维也纳会议中发挥的作用——促使威斯特伐利亚体系成为西方所有国际关系的基础。在其论述外交关系的鸿篇巨制《大外交》（1994）中，基辛格再次回归这些主题，同时还广泛讨论了美国的外交政策。2011年，基辛格出版了《论中国》，着重阐述了中美关系的历史并就美国应该如何应对中国这个超级大国的崛起提出了建议。换言之，在《世界秩序》中讨论的一大半主题，基辛格之前都写过。

《世界秩序》的原创性并不是来自他构建其叙事的材料，而是在于他如何运用这些信息表明世界秩序的概念并不是西方独有的。

---

1. 亨利·基辛格：《世界秩序》，纽约：企鹅出版社，2015年，第2页。

第二部分：学术思想

5 思想主脉

要点 🗝

- 《世界秩序》的主题是世界秩序、权力和合法性,基辛格借助这些主题考察了欧洲、伊斯兰、亚洲和美国的世界秩序概念。
- 亨利·基辛格认为,秩序需要通过外交的方式加以培养,而不是通过军事力量强加于人。
- 该书故意采用了通俗易懂的风格,意在同时吸引普通读者和专业人士。该书绝不是枯燥的学术著作。

核心主题

亨利·基辛格《世界秩序》的主题已蕴含在其标题中:世界秩序本身、权力和合法性。《世界秩序》考察了世界各地的历史经历如何造就了欧洲、伊斯兰、亚洲和美国对于这些观念的截然不同的认识。

最具主导地位的世界秩序观是欧洲的世界秩序观,它源自欧洲三十年战争(1618—1648)结束后于17世纪形成的威斯特伐利亚秩序。1648年签署的威斯特伐利亚和约结束了冲突,引入了均势和主权的概念。

伊斯兰的世界秩序观具有普遍性,其权力和合法性源自宗教。这种观点认为,伊斯兰注定会扩张到非信徒的区域,直到全世界都纳入基于先知穆罕默德*教义的统一体系中。[1]

亚洲秩序则体现出多样性*,中国、日本和印度构建的秩序互相竞争。中国自认为是一种等级分明、具有普遍性的秩序观的中心。正如基辛格所言,"不存在欧洲意义上的主权,因为皇帝统御'天下'。"[2] 然而,日本脱离中国独自构建了秩序,虽然它不可避免地受到比其大得多的邻国的影响。在日本,合法性归天皇所有,他是神圣的,是"天子"。然而,第二次世界大战后,日本基本上采用了威斯特伐利亚的权力和合法性概念。与此类似,印度的文化根植于印度教,而不是中国的儒家思想,因此印度渴望一种基于互相尊重、互不侵犯、互不干涉、平等互利和和平共处的多极*世界秩序——一种由几个差不多实力的国家主导的世界秩序。[3]

最后,美国意义上的世界秩序观源于欧洲,但经过了修正,考虑到了自由、公正和美国例外主义*(这种思想认为,美国与其他国家的不同之处主要在于基于自由、公正和代议制民主的意识形态)的概念:"美国人的世界秩序观认为,一旦其他民族像美国人一样获得了自治权,和平和均势就会自然降临,昔日的宿敌也会捐弃前嫌。"[4]

> "世界秩序反映了一个地区或一种文明对它认为放之四海而皆准的公正安排和实力分布的本质所持的理念。国际秩序是指在世界上很大一部分地区——大到足以影响全球均势——应用这些理念。区域秩序是指同样的原则用于某一具体的地理区域。"
>
> ——亨利·基辛格:《世界秩序:反思国家特征和历史进程》

思想探究

欧洲的世界秩序观形成于 17 世纪,当时整个欧洲大陆旷日持久的战争已经结束。正如基辛格解释说,威斯特伐利亚体系"以一个由独立国家组成的体系为基础,各国不干涉彼此的内部事务,并通过大体上的均势遏制各自的野心。"[5] 每个国家对一块地理区域行使主权(即实施统治的权力和能力)并"把其他国家的国内结构和宗教追求当作现实加以接受,不再试图挑战它们的存在。"[6] 最后,如果一个国家强于其他国家,那么其他国家就会组成一个联盟,它们整合的力量可以让它们恢复均势。

伊斯兰秩序源于 7 世纪,穆罕默德在公元 632 年去世后,伊斯兰教从阿拉伯腹地大幅扩张。在 100 年间,伊斯兰的军队征服了大片领土,从西面的直布罗陀海峡(北非和西班牙南部之间的海峡)到东面的印度次大陆部分地区。基辛格评论说,"伊斯兰教既是一种宗教,又是一个多族裔的超级国家和一种新的世界秩序。"[7] 对于居住在这些伊斯兰教领土——称为"达尔·阿勒·伊斯兰"或者说"伊斯兰之家"——内的人而言,他们有责任将居住在"伊斯兰之家"以外地区——"达尔·阿勒·哈珀"或者说"征伐之地"——的非穆斯林人民融入伊斯兰帝国中。实现这一普世世界秩序观的策略就是所谓的圣战*(意为"斗争"——尽管通常被误解为"圣战")。

亚洲的世界秩序观是最古老的。公元前 221 年统一后,中国一直位于亚洲秩序的中心。中国自认是"世界上唯一的主权政府"——即"天下",其皇帝是"连接凡间和神界的关键人物"。[8] "按照这一观点,"基辛格指出,"世界秩序反映的是全球的等级制,而不是互相竞争的主权国家之间的平衡,"[9] 所有其他国家必须朝贡。换言之,中国的皇帝是神在世间的唯一代表,统御世界上的所有国家。

最后，美国的秩序观规避了传统威斯特伐利亚的均势观和等级观，支持基于民主、公正和自由原则的普世秩序观。"天定命运"*是指 19 世纪普遍认可的信条，即美国注定会从大西洋向西扩张到太平洋。关于"天定命运"，基辛格指出："美国在世界秩序问题上扮演了矛盾的角色：它以天定命运之名在整个美洲大陆扩张，却宣称绝无帝国企图；对重大事件发挥着决定性影响，却矢口否认有国家利益的动机；最终成为超级大国，却声言无意施行强权政治。"因此，美国的世界秩序观有点理想主义，以传播"自认为其他所有民族都渴望照搬的"价值观为基础。[10]

语言表述

《世界秩序》是一部商业化的作品，面向广大读者，因而语言风格通俗易懂，意在吸引普通读者，同时又吸引尽可能多的专业人士和其他专家。这并不意味着书中的语言或者探讨的思想不够深刻。然而，与其先前的作品，比如 1994 年出版、为专业人士量身打造的《大外交》相比，《世界秩序》更像基辛格 2011 年的作品《论中国》，特意面向更广大的读者群。

现已年过九旬的基辛格在书中承认，他有研究助理帮自己开展研究工作并打出书稿，也坦承主流商业出版商企鹅出版社对书稿进行了大量细致的编辑工作，企鹅出版社必定希望该作品能够获得尽可能多的读者。他指出，许多同事、学者、事实核查员、熟人和朋友读过书稿并提出了编辑意见。[11] 总而言之，由于这些因素，《世界秩序》比他的许多其他作品更加清晰易懂。

1. 亨利·基辛格:《世界秩序》,纽约:企鹅出版社,2015年,第5页。
2. 基辛格:《世界秩序》,第4—5页。
3. 基辛格:《世界秩序》,第205页。
4. 基辛格:《世界秩序》,第6页。
5. 基辛格:《世界秩序》,第3页。
6. 基辛格:《世界秩序》,第3页。
7. 基辛格:《世界秩序》,第99页。
8. 基辛格:《世界秩序》,第213页。
9. 基辛格:《世界秩序》,第213页。
10. 基辛格:《世界秩序》,第234页。
11. 基辛格:《世界秩序》,第375—377页。

6. 思想支脉

要点

- 《世界秩序》的次要思想是均势（或者说力量平衡）、主权（行使权力的权利）和国家利益（一个国家认为对其政治、军事、经济或外交声誉或其生存至关重要的东西）。
- 由于欧洲通过殖民主义*（抢占领土并对其实行统治以获取经济和政治利益的政策）将占主导地位的国际体系强加给世界，这些威斯特伐利亚的概念对于理解国际关系如何运作至关重要。
- 基辛格认为技术的影响正在改变新世界秩序的萌生。

其他思想

亨利·基辛格《世界秩序》的次级主题是主权、均势和国家利益，这些概念对于基辛格的核心主题——普遍世界秩序（他认为这一秩序从未真正存在过）——至关重要。他还指出了世界领导人在寻求构建新世界秩序时所面临的核心挑战。

主权概念是指一位统治者、一个国家或一个民族享有统治其公民或另一个国家的公民或控制一个地理区域的权力。决定主权的一个关键因素是统治者或政府在特定区域享有的权力得到其他国家的认可。

外交事务中的一个重要概念是均势，或者说"力量平衡"。比如，在国际关系的现实主义者学派看来，如果世界上的所有国家拥有完全相同的军事能力，战争就不太可能发生，因为任何一个国家都无法击败另一个国家；这样，一种均势就会出现。如若不然，按照这种理论，如果一个国家相对于其他国家获得了优势，其他国家就会团结一致挑战那个强大的国家并重建平衡。

《世界秩序》的另一个核心概念是国家利益：一个国家认为对其持续生存至关重要并试图实现的目标。比如，美国的经济依靠进口的外国石油。如果一个敌对的实体，无论是国家还是恐怖组织，控制这些石油来源，就可能使美国的经济瘫痪。因此，防止这样的敌对实体控制石油供应，同时建设自身的石油产业以减少对外国石油的依赖，属于美国的国家利益。

基辛格指出，近年来，传统的威斯特伐利亚国家观受到了攻击、侵蚀或者拆解。第二个挑战是世界的政治组织和经济组织互不协调：经济体系已经实现全球化，但各个国家并没有实现全球化。最后一项挑战是缺少一个有效的机制让世界大国在重要问题上磋商和合作。[1]

> "唯有威斯特伐利亚原则被普遍认为是构成世界秩序的基础。"
> ——亨利·基辛格：《世界秩序：反思国家特征和历史进程》

思想探究

威斯特伐利亚和约被认为是世界历史上的一个重大转折点。这是连续三个不同的协议，签署于1648年，结束了极具破坏性的三十年战争（1618—1648）。正如基辛格所言，在该和约基础上衍生的主权概念即包含"每个（国家）享有不受外来干涉选择本国制度和宗教信仰的权利"。[2] 此外，"如果一国能（接受）这些基本要求，它就能被接纳为国际社会的成员，继续保持自己的文化、政治、宗教以及国内政策,并得到国际体系的保护,不受外来干涉。"³ 这种国际社会的成员身份——及对该成员身份的认可——是国际体系的支架,建立在统治者或者国家对其管辖的区域行使主权的理念之上。

1648 年的威斯特伐利亚协议带来的和平建立了欧洲的均势。基辛格解释说:"任何国际秩序……迟早要达到均势,否则就会陷入无休止的战乱之中。"因此,为了避免这种结果,欧洲政治家认为各国的军事和经济均势是外交政策的主要目标。基辛格指出了均势会受到挑战的两种路径:第一种路径是,当一个二流国家试图"跻身列强行列,从而导致其他大国采取一系列应对措施,直到达成新的平衡";第二种路径是,当一个大国的实力提升到足以威胁均势的水平时。⁴ 第一种路径的一个绝佳例子是 1871 年的德意志统一*,随后 1879 年又与奥地利-匈牙利结成同盟,导致欧洲均势失衡。到了 1907 年,这一威胁促使英国、法国和俄罗斯形成被称为"三国协约"*的同盟,对抗德国和奥地利-匈牙利的军事联盟。同盟国(主要是英国、苏联和美国)的集体回应导致纳粹德国在第二次世界大战中战败则是第二种路径的一个绝佳例子。

最后,基辛格认为每个政府的职责就是保护其国家利益。他意识到一个国家的利益并不总是与其盟友或敌人的利益相符。他援引 19 世纪英国首相巴麦尊勋爵*的话说:"国家之间没有永恒的盟友,也没有永恒的敌人,只有永恒的利益。我们的义务就是维护这些利益。"⁵ 换言之,政府需要竭尽全力实现其目标,无论是通过外交手段、秘密行动还是战争。

被忽视之处

由于《世界秩序》出版于 2014 年,学者尚无机会详细论证基辛格提出的思想和主题。当然，随着时间推移，由于世界局势还将持续影响我们对世界秩序这一概念的理解，这一切会有所改观。

或许今后几年依然会被学者忽视的一个方面是基辛格论述"技术与世界秩序之间关系"的章节。这一章源于基辛格与一位同事的对话，几乎像是后来添加上去的。然而，它可能是该书所有章节中最具有原创性的一章，因为它展现了人类如何进入一个技术推动的新时代。正如基辛格解释道，"（每个）时代有一套解读世界的信念。科学技术是我们这个时代的主导观念。"[6] 的确，自从第二次世界大战和计算机开发以来，科学技术开启了主要由技术推动的新时代：网络时代（即由计算机推动的信息时代）。基辛格认为，这一新时代有可能同时给世界秩序观带来积极和消极的革命性变革。尽管该书的大部分读者会关注基辛格对世界秩序不同角度的考察，但这是一个可能被忽视的方面。

---

1. 亨利·基辛格：《世界秩序》，纽约：企鹅出版社，2015年，第369—370页。
2. 基辛格：《世界秩序》，第26页。
3. 基辛格：《世界秩序》，第27页。
4. 基辛格：《世界秩序》，第33页。
5. 基辛格：《世界秩序》，第27—30页。
6. 基辛格：《世界秩序》，第330页。

7 历史成就

要点

- 亨利·基辛格成功地表明了欧洲、伊斯兰、亚洲和美国的世界秩序观如何因不同的历史经历而走上了不同的道路。
- 令《世界秩序》大获成功的最重要因素是基辛格的声望和渊博的世界历史知识。
- 唯一可能限制该书成功的因素是基辛格似乎在富有争议的问题（比如伊朗的核计划）上采取了有失公允的立场。

观点评价

毫无疑问,亨利·基辛格的《世界秩序:反思国家特征和历史进程》成功地实现了其目标。基辛格基本上按照区域来组织其章节,以通俗易懂的方式将几个世纪的历史编织在一起,展现了各个区域各自如何理解世界秩序、主权和合法性以及如何达到均势。该书开篇讨论了这些核心概念,然后概述了世界历史,首先论述了欧洲历史和威斯特伐利亚体系的发展。

该书随后论述了伊斯兰秩序的起源,讨论了伊朗在中东非同寻常的地位。伊朗既是一个古老的国家（波斯）,拥有与欧洲交流的悠久历史,又是最大的什叶派*穆斯林国家——什叶派是伊斯兰教两大教派之一,逊尼派*是另一个教派。接着,基辛格分析了亚洲的多极政治,细致考察了日本和印度的世界秩序观。他紧接着详细探讨了中国的世界秩序观。

在第 7 章和第 8 章中,基辛格采用历史分析与传统论述相结合的方法考察了美国历史，关注了西奥多·罗斯福和伍德罗·威尔逊*等美国总统及其在塑造美国世界秩序观中发挥的作用。他也重点论述了美国如何在冷战结束后成为唯一的超级大国。最后，基辛格另辟一章论述了技术在塑造未来世界秩序中的作用，主要论述了技术在改变各国交流方式的同时引发了新的威胁。

阅读《世界秩序》能够相当清晰地感受到基辛格实现了总体目标：表明了从未存在过真正的全球性世界秩序，并提出，如果要构建一种普世的世界秩序观，许多挑战有待应对。

> "如果你觉得美国干得不错，请直接跳到诗歌评论。然而，要是你对渐渐失控的全球忧心忡忡，那么《世界秩序》适合你。该书融合了历史、地理和现代政治，激情澎湃……（这）是一位著名怀疑论者的大声疾呼，是一位熟谙历史的老者对后世的警告。"
>
> ——约翰·米可斯维特："当世界转向时：亨利·基辛格的'世界秩序'"，《纽约时报》

当时的成就

《世界秩序》（2014）的出版正值国际政治混乱期。2014年一整年里，地缘政治对全球秩序的挑战在世界范围内层出不穷。在中东，叙利亚内战陷入困境，叙利亚政府、美国和沙特支持的军事力量和自称为伊拉克和大叙利亚伊斯兰国（ISIS）的激进武装团体之间出现了三重冲突。相当出人意料的是，2014年6月，伊斯兰国成功攻占了叙利亚和伊拉克的大片领土，包括伊拉克的第二大城市摩苏尔。在亚洲，中国开始展示其军事和经济实力，尤其在中国南海群岛上。与此同时，世界目光聚集在马航370*的神秘失踪上；

迄今为止，其失踪的原因尚未完全得到清楚解释。在东欧，乌克兰的抗议触发了紧张关系，导致俄罗斯支持的政府被推翻。在混乱中，俄罗斯吞并了克里米亚半岛（黑海北岸的一块领土，又称为克里木），内战爆发。2014年3月，西非爆发埃博拉病毒*，导致近2.5万人丧生，这引发了进一步动荡。[1]

当年9月《世界秩序》出版时，德国外交家沃尔夫冈·伊申格尔在书评中指出，"称《世界秩序》适逢其时是一种低估，如果说2014年世界渴望一样东西，那就是秩序。"[2] 另一位书评人把该书描述成一部"人们急需的作品"，可以"作为备忘录供后世的决策者使用，让他们知道管理接下来的半个世纪不会比最近这半个世纪更容易。"[3]

局限性

《世界秩序》是否会对学术圈内外有关如何构建一种世界秩序（如果有的话）的当前辩论产生影响？目前下定论还为时尚早。但必须指出的是，由于《世界秩序》广泛论述了世界历史，该书在空间和时间方面都没有局限性；据此可以认为，它在可预见的未来都具有价值，尽管其中提到的伊拉克和大叙利亚伊斯兰国的兴起及俄罗斯对乌克兰的干预等事件都是2014年最新出现的。

然而，鉴于基辛格成年后都在拥护和践行美国的外交政策，该书明显表现出支持美国的态度并不令人意外。在其论述美伊关系的章节中尤其如此。在那一章中，他表示，在其与联合国安理会*的五个常任理事国（中国、法国、俄罗斯、英国和美国）和德国谈判期间，伊朗在获取核武器方面取得了快速进展。[4] 然而，这种看法纯属揣测，没有事实依据：既没有证据表明伊朗寻求发展核武器，也没有证据表明它在获取核武器方面取得了进展。另有证据表明，伊朗的核能力在谈判期间大大减弱了。[5] 不过，基辛格对于伊斯兰崛起的历史论述与其论述亚洲的章节一样，既发人深省又准确中肯。换言之，基辛格支持美国的偏见并不会完全减弱这部作品的价值。

---

1. 沃尔夫冈·伊申格尔："基辛格的世界：如何维护全球秩序"，《外交》，2014年3/4月，登录日期2015年10月1日，https://www.foreignaffairs.com/reviews/2015-03-01/world-according-kissinger。
2. 伊申格尔："基辛格的世界"。
3. 拉纳·米特："评亨利·基辛格的'世界秩序'"，《卫报》，2014年10月1日，登录日期2015年11月4日，https://www.theguardian.com/books/2014/oct/01/world-order-by-henry-kissinger-review-account。
4. 亨利·基辛格：《世界秩序》，纽约：企鹅出版社，2015年，第159页。
5. 美国武器控制协会："伊朗核谈判：明辨是非"，《协会简报》第7卷，2015年1月第2期，登录日期2015年11月4日，https://www.armscontrol.org/issue-briefs/2015-01-23/Iran-Nuclear-Negotiations-Separating-Myth-from-Reality。

8 著作地位

要点

- 亨利·基辛格的一生都在研究和参与全球政治。这个主题贯穿他的全部作品。
- 《世界秩序》是一位年长的学者、外交家和政治家的作品,因而体现了对知识的深刻认识和多年的治国经验。
- 《世界秩序》可能是基辛格最后的著作。

定位

亨利·基辛格的《世界秩序:反思国家特征和历史进程》在其漫长又相当成功的学术和政治生涯的晚期面世。在 1957 年至 2015 年间,他出版了 14 部学术著作和 3 部回忆录,叙述了他在政府担任国家安全顾问和在理查德·尼克松总统和杰拉尔德·福特总统任职期间担任国务卿的经历。因此,《世界秩序》是一位成熟思想家的作品,他一生的大部分时间都用于思考权力、国际舞台上国家间的均势和世界秩序问题。

基辛格一直是现实政治*的坚定拥护者,现实政治认为政策决定应该以务实为考量,而不是以道德或者意识形态为考量。这一点在其著作和白宫任职期间采取的行动中显而易见。例如,1972 年,对冷战均持强硬"主战"态度的基辛格和尼克松制定了一个以削弱苏联实力来增强美国实力的战略。他们意识到莫斯科与北京的关系已经恶化,于是重启了与中国的外交关系,迫使苏联在通常所称的"缓和"*(1969 年至 1979 年间,美国采取的一项与苏联缓和紧张关系的政策）期间同意了一系列双边（双向）协议。这一举动是一次出其不意的重大外交胜利，让美国改善了与苏联和中国的关系，同时又让自己从血腥的越南战争中抽身。

> "美国人喜欢牛仔……独自一人，一路骑着马走进城镇，走进乡村，除了他的马，再无其他……这一神奇而浪漫的角色与我完全相符，因为享受孤独总是我风格的一部分，也可以说是我技能的一部分。"
>
> —— 亨利·基辛格：《白宫岁月》

整合

从基辛格的作品整体来看，《世界秩序》很可能是其最后的著作；现已92岁高龄的他还在出版作品，令人赞叹。显而易见的是，有一条贯穿其作品的主线：研究国际事务中的权力和秩序。

比如，改编自其博士论文的第一部作品《重建的世界》(1957)主要关注了1815年法国皇帝拿破仑·波拿巴战败后，欧洲新均势是如何在维也纳会议上建立起来的。然而，引起决策者和公众注意的是他的第二部作品《核武器与外交政策》(1957)。在该作品中，基辛格将政治军事思想与有限战争*的理念融合到了一起，由此成为外交政策评论界的领军人物，进而开启了外交家和政治家的生涯。[1] 同样，基辛格的这部作品关注的是，在政治、经济和军事方面存在很大不确定的时期如何创建秩序。

在20世纪60年代，基辛格创作了更多作品，巩固了其作为公共学者的地位。在这些作品中，《选择的必要》(1961)认为要用常规力量灵活应对苏联的挑衅，《麻烦的伙伴关系》(1965)重新评估了美国与其欧洲盟友的关系，刚好在他入驻白宫前出版的《美国的外交政策：论文三篇》（1969）阐述了他对影响美国外交政策制定的一些重要因素有什么看法。

离职后，基辛格出版了多部讲述其在职岁月的回忆录：《白宫岁月》（1979）、《动乱年代》（1982）以及更晚时期的《复兴年代》（1999）。在20世纪八九十年代，基辛格主要出版了论文集、声明以及他任职期间的解密文本。1994年，他出版了一部巨作《大外交》，论述了几百年的宏伟外交史，这或许是他迄今为止为外交研究作出的最大贡献。

近年来，他又转向了学术研究，出版了分析中国外交政策史的《论中国》（2011）和《世界秩序》（2014）。两者都主要关注外交史和世界秩序观。

意义

总体而言，基辛格对外交史和外交政策的研究作出了重大贡献。他以坚定支持"利益为重"的外交政策著称，通过实际分析特定情况下的事实来制定外交政策，这需要将其置身于历史语境中加以理解。

《世界秩序》是体现其观点的一个完美例子。在该作品中，基辛格为读者提供了有关四大世界秩序观成因的宝贵见解并解释了这些世界秩序观之间的差异。当然，这需要大量的研究、知识和共情。通常，对于不熟悉世界其他地区及其历史的人而言，理解其他地区的观点很难。在《世界秩序》中，基辛格以通俗易懂的方式传达了这些观点；比如，对于关注中东事态变化的人而言，"伊斯兰主义与中东"那一章全面描述了伊斯兰教如何在7世纪成为一支强大的力量，同时又深入公允地探讨了现代伊斯兰意识形态的起源，并未掺杂半点敌意。

---

1. 汉斯·摩根索："评亨利·A.基辛格的《核武器与外交政策》",《美国政治学评论》第 50 卷，1958 年 9 月第 3 期，第 842 页。

第三部分：学术影响

9 最初反响

要点

- 《世界秩序》因其对世界秩序的争论作出贡献而备受称赞,但是因基辛格没有批判性地评估乔治·W. 布什或者贝拉克·奥巴马等在世的总统而受到诟病。
- 该书出版于 2014 年,还没有足够的时间引发一场辩论来形成对它的回应。
- 影响《世界秩序》接受度的最重要因素是基辛格富有争议的名声,即那些讨厌他的人撰写的负面评论和那些赞同他的人作出的积极评价。

批评

因为《世界秩序:反思国家特征和历史进程》由极富争议的基辛格所著,它必定会受到许多主流媒体和美国外交政策精英人士的评价。基辛格常被斥为不讲情面的现实主义者,又因在职期间的决策被控在多个国家侵犯人权,[1] 因此,许多人出于个人或者意识形态的原因讨厌他。然而,大多数评论都是相当积极的。比如,美国前国务卿希拉里·克林顿*——一位与基辛格在国际关系领域信奉不同政治哲学的政治家——写道,《世界秩序》"是基辛格的最佳代表作,完美融合了广度和敏锐度,展现了其以点带面、点面结合的技能。"[2]

尽管如此,由于基辛格在《世界秩序》中拒不评论在世的总统,尤其是乔治·W. 布什,人们对此多有诟病。有关书评——比如《经济学人》的一篇书评——特别反对他"用称赞来掩饰对在世政客的批评,这或许为了避免当事人的尴尬"。³ 例如,基辛格没有公正地评论布什政府对伊拉克战争﹡的处理,反而写道:"我想再次对(布什)表示我一如既往的尊敬和欣赏。他在一段风雨飘摇的时期,以勇气、尊严和信仰领导着美国。"⁴ 在提到前美国总统伍德罗·威尔逊——他因在第一次世界大战﹡后的欧洲重建中发挥了作用而广为人知——时,记者詹姆斯·特拉布﹡表达了与《经济学人》类似的看法,指出他简直不敢相信基辛格会"对他们当中最鲁莽的威尔逊(理想主义者)乔治·W.布什大加赞赏。"⁵

> "《世界秩序》是一部应该与每个国会议员一起关在房间里的作品——他们在宣誓就职前必须先阅读它。"
>
> ——约翰·米可斯维特:"当世界转向时:亨利·基辛格的'世界秩序'",《纽约时报》

回应

基辛格不太可能回应对《世界秩序》的评论,这有几个原因。首先,该书出版于2014年9月,因而尚无大量时间供学界探讨这个话题,主要是因为学术书评要通过同行评审过程得花一年多时间。

其次,作为一个重要的公众人物,基辛格往往不会像常人一样回应评论,尤其不会回应诸如国际关系学者安妮-玛丽·斯劳特等个人的评论,他和安妮-玛丽·斯劳特在意识形态方面存在分歧。回应评论不是他的风格,基辛格是那种出版了作品,随后周游世界,在享有盛名的大学和机构开公共讲座的学者,这类讲座通常经过精心策划，所提的问题有一定尖锐性但又没有明显敌意。

最后一个基辛格不太可能回应该书评论的原因是他年事已高，即便面对最有说服力的反方观点，他也不太可能改变自己的观点了。因此，基辛格和其评论者之间有关该书的批判性对话似乎不太可能发生。

冲突与共识

该书出版的一项较为确定的学术成果是推进现实主义者和理想主义者（他们拥有不同的世界秩序观）之间的辩论。像基辛格这样的现实主义者认为外交政策必须在合法性的基础上彰显实力。比如，2003年，美国主导了伊拉克入侵行动，导致了伊拉克战争；尽管基辛格支持该行动，认为2001年9月11日恐怖袭击（911事件）之后，美国需要投射其实力，但他也意识到伊拉克缺乏大规模杀伤性武器*的事实破坏了这次维护治安行动的合法性。简而言之，实力本身还不够，还必须是合法的。对于许多赞同基辛格的世界观的人而言，实力投射胜过任何倡导合作的理想主义观点。

现实主义者和理想主义者之间争论的实质也正是这个问题。比如，安妮-玛丽·斯劳特完全不认可基辛格的作品，这反映了她将合法性置于投射实力之上的观点。在她看来，外交政策必须建立在道德考量之上，绝对不能以牺牲合法性为代价。她认为国家不仅有责任保护国内的公民，还有责任保护世界各地的公民；如有必要，国家应该采取行动防止暴行，像那些发生在叙利亚的暴行。[6]

这两大阵营之间的分歧无法轻易调和，将继续主导今后美国外交政策的辩论。

1. 丹尼尔·马兰斯："亨利·基辛格刚到92岁。他对自己走向何方小心翼翼原因就在此"，《赫芬顿邮报》，2015年5月27日，登录日期2015年10月9日，https://www.huffingtonpost.com/2015/05/27/henry-kissinger-human-rights_n_7454172.html。
2. 希拉里·克林顿："希拉里·克林顿评亨利·基辛格的《世界秩序》"，《华盛顿邮报》，2014年9月4日，登录日期2015年9月18日，https://www.washingtonpost.com/opinions/hillary-clinton-reviews-henry-kissingers-world-order/2014/09/04/b280c654-31ea-11e4-8f02-03c644b2d7d0_story.html。
3. 《经济学人》："有点混乱"，2014年9月6日，登录日期2015年9月10日，https://www.economist.com/news/books-and-arts/21615478-geopolitics-henry-kissinger-grand-and-gloomy-bit-of-a-mess。
4. 亨利·基辛格：《世界秩序》，纽约：企鹅出版社，2015年，第325页。
5. 詹姆斯·特拉布："书评：亨利·基辛格的《世界秩序》"，《华尔街日报》，2014年9月5日，登录日期2015年9月18日，https://www.wsj.com/articles/book-review-world-order-by-henry-kissinger-1409952751。
6. 安妮-玛丽·斯劳特："如何修正美国的外交政策"，《新共和》，2014年11月19日，登录日期2015年9月18日，https://newrepublic.com/article/120030/world-order-review-what-obama-should-learn-kissingers-book。

10 后续争议

要 点

- 《世界秩序》给如何构建新世界秩序的辩论带来了什么？目前下定论还为时尚早。该书与其说提出了一个深刻的观点，还不如说讲解了一个概念的历史。
- 《世界秩序》直接考察了两个主要学派——现实主义和自由国际主义——的思想，同时借鉴了两者的观点。
- 虽然刚出版时引起了热烈反响，但《世界秩序》还未对世界秩序的辩论产生重大影响。

应用与问题

作为自20世纪50年代以来美国外交政策领域的一个主导声音，亨利·基辛格在《世界秩序：反思国家特征和历史进程》中表达的思想是其一生学术研究、深刻思考和辩论的产物。该书是对世界秩序这一重要主题的分析，出自一位备受尊重又富有影响力的政治家之手，可谓适逢其时，丰富了当前关于在充满混乱的世界中如何构建一种秩序的辩论。

由于该书于2014年9月刚刚出版，判断基辛格将如何进一步完善其在书中所提出的思想还为时尚早。随着该书的出版，有关如何以最好的方式构建一种可行的新世界秩序的辩论并没有减少，自由国际主义者认为要加强国际机构的力量，而现实主义者寻求实力投射，通常是付诸武力。更麻烦的是，美国有些派别，比如新保守派人士*——这些人信奉强调自由市场资本主义和干涉主义外交政策的政治哲学——极力反对自由国际主义，并致力于破坏自由国际主义者试图建设的机构。

尽管基辛格如何构建新世界秩序的立场往往更接近自由派的理解，但他依然是投射美国实力的倡导者。基辛格在今后几年是否会在接下来出版的作品中进一步探讨这一立场，值得期待。

> "以价值观为基础的外交政策可以非常务实和谨慎。参与弊显然大于利的活动毫无意义。"
>
> —— 安妮-玛丽·斯劳特：
> "如何修正美国的外交政策"，《新共和》

思想流派

基辛格早已是国际关系学者（特别是那些关注美国外交政策的学者）之间辩论的关键人物，在这场辩论中，现实主义者和理想主义者针锋相对。这两派的思想非常广泛，各自融合了几个分支，本身就互相对立。在这两派中，基辛格显然是现实主义的大力支持者，但只要对他在《世界秩序》中提出的思想进行更为细致的考察，就可以看出他实际上可能代表着两者之间的桥梁。正如美国前国务卿希拉里·克林顿在其对《世界秩序》的正面评论中指出，基辛格认为一种国际秩序要想屹立不倒，"它必须将'实力与合法性'联系起来。"在她看来，这个观点"听上去惊人的理想主义"。[1] 她说得不错。尽管基辛格自称是一名现实主义者，但他认为美国在维护他认同的美国价值观——自由、公正和民主——和世界秩序观时最为强大。

在基辛格看来，美国政策的一个重要目标应该是构建一种"肯定个人尊严和参与式治理、遵照一致同意的规则开展国际合作的世界秩序"。[2] 尽管这是一个相当理想主义的目标,但基辛格并不天真;他意识到构建新世界秩序的过程充满了挑战,其中一些挑战可能需要付诸武力。虽然理想主义者不再质疑这种观点,但如今的真正争议点在于在什么样的情况下应该使用武力。一方面,安妮-玛丽·斯劳特等现代理想主义者认为,当政府无法保护其公民时,应该遵循保护责任(R2P)*的原则(在国际关系中,根据这个原则,一个无法保护其公民免受人权侵犯的国家会丧失其主权,这意味着国际社会有权进行干预)使用武力。另一方面,基辛格认为,当一国的国家利益受到威胁,而外交努力无法达成协议时,应该使用武力。

当代研究

尽管基辛格在美国外交政策精英中有很多拥趸,其中甚至包括与他意见相左的人,比如比尔·克林顿,但我们不能说《世界秩序》出版后很快围绕该书形成了一派思想或者带来了一群追随者。然而,这并不意味着《世界秩序》与其他现实主义者的作品格格不入,像国际关系学者法里德·扎卡利亚*和约翰·米尔斯海默这样的现实主义者也经常从历史的角度透视美国外交政策中的权力、合法性和国家利益的问题。

比如,2013年6月,扎卡利亚上传了一个视频,将叙利亚内战置于历史语境中。他指出,继黎巴嫩内战*(1975—1990)和2003年美国领导的入侵伊拉克之后,叙利亚是中东三个少数派执政的国家中最后一个痛苦地完成向多数派执政过渡的国家;他还警告称,解决叙利亚的悲剧至少需要十年时间。他借助历史表达了反对美国干预叙利亚的观点，因为推翻现政权会引发无数派别间的权力争斗，其中伊拉克和大叙利亚伊斯兰国（ISIS）是最强大的。³

对于 2014 年乌克兰*政府倒台和随后俄罗斯吞并克里米亚半岛带来的危机，米尔斯海默给出了类似的解释。米尔斯海默不赞同"该危机是俄罗斯侵略的产物"的传统观点，表示"美国及其欧洲的盟友要为这次危机负主要责任"，因为他们的策略是不顾俄罗斯领导人的一再反对，将乌克兰纳入西方的轨道。⁴

---

1. 希拉里·克林顿："希拉里·克林顿评亨利·基辛格的《世界秩序》"，《华盛顿邮报》，2014 年 9 月 4 日，登录日期 2015 年 9 月 18 日，https://www.washingtonpost.com/opinions/hillary-clinton-reviews-henry-kissingers-world-order/2014/09/04/b280c654-31ea-11e4-8f02-03c644b2d7d0_story.html。
2. 亨利·基辛格：《世界秩序》，纽约：企鹅出版社，2015 年，第 373 页。
3. 法里德·扎卡利亚："欢迎提问法里德·扎卡利亚：远离叙利亚"，天线网，2013 年 6 月 7 日，登录日期 2015 年 10 月 16 日，http://dish.andrewsullivan.com/2013/06/07/ask-fareed-zakaria-anything-stay-out-of-syria/。
4. 约翰·米尔斯海默："为什么乌克兰危机是西方的错"，《外交》，2014 年 9/10 月，登录日期 2015 年 10 月 16 日，https://www.foreignaffairs.com/articles/russia-fsu/2014-08-18/why-ukraine-crisis-west-s-fault。

11 当代印迹

要点 🗝

- 如今,《世界秩序》脱颖而出,成为世界史和国际政治专业学生的重要入门书。
- 对于基辛格思想的主要质疑来自自由国际主义者,他们认为他没有意识到保护责任原则(根据这个原则,如果一个国家无法保护其公民免受人权侵犯,国际社会就有权进行干预)的重要性。
- 基辛格还没有直接回应该质疑。

地位

作为当代有关"如何构建新世界秩序"辩论的一部分,亨利·基辛格的《世界秩序:反思国家特征和历史进程》为其读者广泛概述了其中的主要问题,但并没有提供精心构思的解决方案。这似乎是有意为之。该书从未打算就美国应该如何在世界其他地方推行其世界秩序观提出一套具体的建议,而是要回顾历史来详细论述后世在构建这样一种新秩序时会面临的挑战。从这个意义上来说,基辛格的作品是理解现代全球政治的重要向导,而不是解决世界上许多问题的药方。

由于这个原因,该作品对于现实主义者(比如基辛格)与自由国际主义者(他们认为加强国际机构是建立新秩序的最佳方式)之间更广泛的辩论有多大重要性,目前尚无共识。尽管基辛格并不反对像联合国这样的国际机构,但其共和党*中新保守派的同事,比如保罗·沃尔福威茨和约翰·博尔顿持不同意见。他们认为美国需要通过武力来维护世界秩序,发动伊拉克战争就是为了达到这个目的。从这个意义上来说,基辛格的作品在左翼的理想主义和多边主义秩序观与右翼的现实主义和单边主义秩序观之间架起了某种桥梁。在基辛格看来,国际机构需要加强,但他也认为,当国家或非国家实体(比如伊拉克和大叙利亚伊斯兰国)威胁到国家利益时,国家保留使用武力的权利。

> "基辛格坚定支持威斯特伐利亚绝对主权原则的讽刺之处——和永远的悲哀之处——在于保护责任实际上是威斯特伐利亚和约的继承者。"
> —— 安妮-玛丽·斯劳特:"如何修正美国的外交政策",《新共和》

互动

作为一部以现实主义构想为前提的作品,《世界秩序》与以合作为前提的自由国际主义者的世界秩序观有点对立。对基辛格的《世界秩序》中所表达的观点最直言不讳的挑战者是安妮-玛丽·斯劳特,她是普林斯顿大学的国际事务教授,担任美国国务院(处理外交事务的政府部门)政策规划司主任。她认为,基辛格信奉的以实力为基础的外交政策没有考虑新世界秩序观建设中的最新进展,在该进展中,一个被称为保护责任(R2P)的相对较新的外交政策概念修正了威斯特伐利亚原则。斯劳特认为,当政府无法保护其公民时,各国有义务依据《世界人权宣言》*进行干预。她对基辛格的抱怨源自他"坚定支持威斯特伐利亚绝对主权原则"。另外,他没有意识到的是"保护责任实际上是威斯特伐利亚和约(1648)的继承者"。

"在一个对无辜平民使用武力的最大威胁通常不是来自外国政府而是来自本国政府的时代里,保护责任是威斯特伐利亚戒条的一个必要修正。它修正了绝对主权的理念,促使各国至少为大屠杀负责。"1

总之,斯劳特认为,基辛格没有意识到一种新的世界秩序已经开始成形,这主要是因为它与他的世界秩序观不符。

持续争议

当前自由派和新保守派在世界秩序观上的争论无法在短时间内结束,因为美国的党派政治加剧了两者之间的理念分歧。最近世界秩序辩论的重点集中于中东,在那里,伊拉克和大叙利亚伊斯兰国的崛起打乱了区域秩序。鉴于危机无法在短时间内解除,基辛格在最近的一篇文章中提出了一套奥巴马政府如何从日益恶化的中东形势中脱身的建议。他写道:"美国的政策迷失在各方错误的意图动机中,因此几乎丧失了影响事态的能力。现在美国与该地区各方都对立或在某些方面有分歧:与埃及是人权问题,与沙特阿拉伯是也门问题,与叙利亚各方存在不同目标。美国声称誓要让叙利亚总统巴沙尔·阿萨德*下台,但又不愿使用有效的政治或军事影响力来实现这个目标。"2

基辛格认为,"只要伊斯兰国存活并控制着一块地理区域,就会加剧中东的所有紧张关系",并称"摧毁伊斯兰国比推翻巴沙尔·阿萨德更加迫切"。这一提议深深根植于基辛格投射美国实力的信念,这种信念也是他抱怨奥巴马政府默许俄罗斯于2015年秋军事干预叙利亚的原因。3

斯劳特的立场与其略有差异。尽管在"美国要在叙利亚有所作为"的问题上，她与基辛格观点一致，但在最终目标上，她与基辛格意见相左。基辛格认为目标是要摧毁伊斯兰国，而斯劳特认为目标应该限于拯救无辜平民，这就是她呼吁美国及其盟友在叙利亚设立"禁飞区"或"安全区"来保护平民并逐步缓解不断升级的人道主义危机的原因。[4]

这两种视角凸显出了现实主义者和自由国际主义者之间的细微差别。

---

1. 安妮-玛丽·斯劳特："如何修正美国的外交政策"，《新共和》，2014 年 11 月 19 日，登录日期 2015 年 9 月 18 日，https://newrepublic.com/article/120030/world-order-review-what-obama-should-learn-kissingers-book。
2. 亨利·基辛格："摆脱中东困境之道"，《华尔街日报》，2015 年 10 月 16 日，登录日期 2015 年 10 月 22 日，https://www.wsj.com/articles/a-path-out-of-the-middle-east-collapse-1445037513。
3. 基辛格："摆脱中东困境之道"。
4. 安妮-玛丽·斯劳特："为叙利亚设立禁飞区"，世界报业辛迪加网站，2015 年 8 月 25 日，登录日期 2015 年 10 月 22 日，https://www.project-syndicate.org/commentary/no-fly-zone-syria-by-anne-marie-slaughter-2015-08。

12 未来展望

要点 🗝

- 《世界秩序》对当前有关世界秩序的本质和如何构建新世界秩序的辩论作出了重要且及时的贡献。
- 展望未来,《世界秩序》将依然是一部重要的作品,因为它让一度停滞却至关重要的世界秩序辩论重新焕发出了活力。
- 重要的是,《世界秩序》在一种全球视野中探讨了有关世界秩序本质的辩论,向读者解释了其他地区存在的世界秩序观。

潜力

亨利·基辛格的《世界秩序：反思国家特征和历史进程》是为那些对过去感兴趣又关注未来的人而写的。该作品为其读者提供了大量有价值的世界历史论述,同时解释了一些世界最伟大文明的起源、细微差别和面临的挑战。这样的论述之所以有价值,正是因为基辛格的这部作品向读者提出了"透彻理解历史是预测未来的最佳方式"的观念。

尽管基辛格似乎不太可能修改或更新该作品,但该作品可能在其他外交历史学家和国际关系学者之间引发一场关于如何创建一种普世的新世界秩序的辩论。这是一块值得年轻学者耕耘的沃土,他们或许对创建如何建立新秩序的理论感兴趣。略有遗憾的是,该书的结论没有提供一个关于该新世界秩序可能是什么的潜在战略——倘若作者给出了可能的选项,这或许会成为其他学者探讨的焦点。然而,随着时间的推移,学界可能会探讨基辛格为何没有提出可能的方案选项。

> "基辛格的秘密愿望可能是要为 21 世纪举办一次维也纳会议。尽管使世界政治变得复杂的许多因素——跨国身份、数字超链接、大规模杀伤性武器和全球恐怖分子网络——已和威斯特伐利亚模式格格不入,但基辛格(在《世界秩序》中)坚信'管理好大国关系依然最为重要'的观点仍然是正确的。"
>
> ——沃尔夫冈·伊申格尔:"基辛格眼中的世界",《外交》

未来方向

目前还难以确定哪些学者(尤其是那些参与世界秩序、主权或均势等广义概念研究的学者)将继承基辛格的衣钵。然而,这样的继承者或继承者们似乎更可能来自国际关系领域而不是外交史领域。这是因为外交历史学家理所当然地关注过去,很少涉及有关未来的概念探讨。这正是基辛格与大多数外交历史学家的不同之处,也是他作为决策者及其随后为世界各地政府担任政治顾问的丰富经验带来的必然副产品。

在国际关系领域,学者们积极从理论层面探讨国家、跨国公司和恐怖组织等非国家成员以及联合国和世界银行等非政府组织间的关系本质。在该领域,有许多理论变体,比如古典现实主义*、新现实主义*、新自由主义*、新古典现实主义*和自由国际主义。其中,新古典现实主义与基辛格的现实政治观最为匹配,专注于权力最大化、保护自身利益而不关心道德问题。鉴于此,希望在基辛格的《世界秩序》的基础上发展理论的学者可能来自该思想学派。在国际关系领域,最有可能的候选人是政治学家约翰·米尔斯海默、斯蒂芬·沃尔特*、罗伯特·卡根*、瓦利·纳斯尔*、弗朗西斯·福山和安妮-玛丽·斯劳特，不过他们每个人几乎肯定会从不同的角度解读问题。

小结

基辛格的《世界秩序》精妙绝伦地深入探讨了当今世界面临的一个核心问题：如何构建一种秩序。该作品敏锐地为读者分析了四种主要的世界秩序观：欧洲的威斯特伐利亚体系，以主权、合法性和均势为前提；普世的伊斯兰秩序观，从历史上看，致使穆斯林教徒和非穆斯林互相争夺主导地位；中国体系，根据这一体系，中国及其权力是其秩序的主要根基；以及美国的秩序观，根植于"自由、公正和民主是适用于全世界的普世价值"的信仰。该书还极其启发性地探讨了技术在促成世界秩序（比如，通过通信网络让人们团结起来）和破坏世界秩序（上传恐怖袭击的视频）中的作用。这种讨论对世界领导人在寻求构建新世界秩序中面临的挑战提供了深刻的见解。

尽管《世界秩序》立足于世界历史，但基辛格用一种独特方式来解释为什么这些秩序观各不相同，这对于任何希望认识当今世界或者关注其未来走向的人都颇具价值。

术语表

1. **911事件**：2001年9月11日，遭伊斯兰激进主义恐怖分子劫持的两架商用客机撞向纽约的世贸中心，导致近3 000人丧生。第三架被劫持的客机撞向了五角大楼，第四架则在宾夕法尼亚州境内坠毁。

2. **阿富汗战争**：美国发生911袭击后，北约及其盟友采取的军事干预。

3. **基地组织**：2001年9月11日，策划向美国发动恐怖袭击的伊斯兰激进主义军事组织。

4. **美国例外主义**：认为美国与其他国家截然不同的一种信仰，主要来源于一种基于自由、公正和代表制民主的意识形态。

5. **无政府状态**：一种无人领导的状态。主权国家就处在一个无政府或自我管理的世界中，没有凌驾于国家之上的权威以这样或那样的方式强迫它们。

6. **专制**：从治理上而言，是一种政府当局干预公民生活、损害公民自由的体制。

7. **均势**：在国际关系领域，一国的实力被另一个国家或另外几个国家的实力制衡的程度。

8. **柏林墙**：1961年至1989年划分柏林的一道障碍，象征着苏联将自己及其卫星国与西方隔离的努力。

9. **博科圣地**：一个伊斯兰军事组织，成立于2002年，在尼日利亚北部活动。自2009年以来，它一直在制造叛乱活动，但直到2014年4月从一所学校绑架了276名女生才引起全球的关注。

10. **资本主义**：一种借助私人商品和服务换取利润的经济体制。

11. **古典现实主义**：一种国际关系理论的学派，认为国家行动是由行为主体驱动的（由领导人而不是体制结构控制），并将人性本不完美视为冲突的来源。

12. **冷战**（1947—1991）：美国及其西方盟友与苏联及其盟友之间的一段紧张时期，以核武器威胁、代理人冲突（即由两国挑起但不直接兵戎相见的冲突）和间谍活动等为特色。

13. **殖民主义**：指一个国家对另一个国家实施完全或部分政治控制并用殖民者占领该国的政策。它通常涉及统治者（殖民者）和被统治者（被殖民者）之间不平等的权力关系和对殖民地的经济掠夺。

14. **共产主义**：一种提倡生产资料国有制、劳动集体制和废除社会阶级的政治意识形态。它是苏联（1922—1991）的意识形态，在冷战期间，与自由市场资本主义形成对比。

15. **儒家思想**：一种由 2 500 年前的中国哲学家孔子创建的亚洲哲学和道德体系。

16. **维也纳会议**（1813—1815）：在最终打败法国皇帝和军事领导人拿破仑·波拿巴前后，在奥地利维也纳举办的一次国际会议，其目的是要在欧洲重建稳定的政治秩序和均势。

17. **达尔·阿勒·哈珀**："征伐之地"，是一个历史术语，指与达尔·阿勒·伊斯兰接壤、需要融入伊斯兰帝国的非穆斯林领土。

18. **达尔·阿勒·伊斯兰**："伊斯兰之家"，即建立于 7 世纪的伊斯兰帝国的领土。

19. **缓和**：1969 年至 1979 年间，美国为应对苏联而实施的一项政策。该政策包括通过减少挑衅行为以及借助会面和峰会增加互动来缓和紧张关系。

20. **东方集团**：指一批社会主义国家，大部分位于东欧，直到 20 世纪 80 年代末才摆脱苏联的统治。

21. **埃博拉病毒爆发**：2014 年，埃博拉病毒的疫情横扫西非，导致近 2.5 万人丧生，在世界各地引发了恐慌。

22. **地缘战略**：研究战略和地理位置塑造政治和国际关系的方式。

23. **《退伍军人权利法案》**：美国在二战期间采用的一项法案，为退伍军

人提供了各种福利，比如提供低利率贷款和奖学金来补贴生活费用和继续教育的学费。

24. **绿色和平组织**：1971 年成立于加拿大，它是一个以非暴力反抗为策略来激发公众和世界领导人环保意识的国际组织。

25. **霸权**：一个单一的国家能够支配所有其他国家的情形。比如，冷战后，美国被认为是全球霸权国家。

26. **印度教**：是一种信奉多神（即信奉的神不止一个）的世界主要宗教，全世界有 10 亿多信徒；其核心区域在印度次大陆。

27. **神圣罗马帝国**：一个由许多国家组成的中欧政治体，形成于中世纪初期，于 19 世纪的头十年解散。

28. **理想主义**：一种国际关系的理论，认为各国应该将本国的哲学应用到处理国际关系上。该理论与美国第 28 任总统、1913 年至 1921 年间执政的伍德罗·威尔逊息息相关，他认为所有人都拥有决定自己命运的权利。

29. **伊朗核计划**：自 20 世纪 90 年代初以来，西方一直指控伊朗研发核武器。伊朗政府一直表示其有权研发和平利用的核技术并否认核武器计划。2003 年以来，各方已就该问题定期举行了多次谈判。

30. **伊拉克战争（2003—2011）**：一场主要发生在美国及其盟友与伊拉克之间的军事冲突。2003 年萨达姆·侯赛因的政府被推翻后，该冲突沦为一场宗派之间的内战，伊拉克的什叶派和逊尼派互相较量。2011 年 12 月，美国军队退出了伊拉克。

31. **伊拉克和大叙利亚伊斯兰国（ISIS）**：一个激进的伊斯兰军事组织，于 2014 年控制了伊拉克和叙利亚的大片领土，同时还在利比亚东部、埃及的西奈半岛以及中东和北非的其他地区活动。

32. **圣战**：伊斯兰教的术语，意指"斗争"。通常误译为圣战，实际上是指与障碍作斗争，无论是与非信徒还是与生活中的各种挑战作斗争。

33. **黎巴嫩内战（1975—1990）**：1975 年中央政权崩溃后，在黎巴嫩发

生的一场冲突。

34. **合法性**：成为合法的或被法律接受的。

35. **自由派**：作为一种政治哲学，自由主义强调个人自由和平等的重要性；它可以追溯至被称为启蒙运动（17 世纪末至 18 世纪末）的欧洲思想大发展时期，那时，压迫人民的世袭统治受到了挑战。

36. **自由国际主义**：一个国际关系的理论学派，认为如果政策倡导构建自由世界秩序的国际结构，各国就可以实现和平和互相合作。

37. **有限战争**：一个用于描述战争类型的军事概念。在有限战争中，战略目标和努力都受限。这个概念通常与全面战争相对，在全面战争中，一个国家可以动用所有资源来战胜对手以确保全面胜利。第二次世界大战是全面战争的最好例子，而 1990 年至 1991 年的海湾战争仅限于迫使伊拉克从科威特撤兵。

38. **马航 370 事件**：2014 年 3 月 8 日，一架从马来西亚首都吉隆坡起飞的飞机失踪，引发了史上最大的搜寻行动之一。没有找到任何幸存者，一年多后才发现一小块残骸。

39. **天定命运**：19 世纪，美国提出的一种信条，用于为该国在北美向西扩张辩护。

40. **多边主义**：三个或三个以上国家一起朝一个目标努力。与双边（两个国家之间）或单边（只有一个国家）相对。

41. **多样性**：这个概念用于描述在某一特定区域存在多极权力的情形（比如，在亚洲，俄罗斯、中国、印度和日本都是权力中心）。

42. **多极性**：国际体系中的一种权力分配；在多极体系中，权力集中在三个或三个以上的国家手里。在两极体系中，权力集中在两个国家手里；在单极体系中，一个国家占据主导地位（又称为霸权）。

43. **确保互相毁灭**：冷战期间使用的一个词组，用于描述如下观点：一个超级大国对另一个超级大国发起进攻会导致双方一同毁灭，因为第一次袭击后，每一方都有能力借助装载核武器的战斗机或潜艇发起报复性的攻击。

44. **国家利益**：国际关系中的一个概念，用于描述一个国家认为对于其政治、军事、经济、外交声誉或生存至关重要的东西。

45. **国家安全顾问**：国家安全、外交政策和防御等相关问题的美国总统总顾问。

46. **纳粹德国**（1933—1945）：阿道夫·希特勒统治下的德国。希特勒是一位极端民族主义的政治家，试图将所有说德语的人统一为一个国家并改变欧洲和全球的秩序。希特勒咄咄逼人和反犹太主义的政策导致了第二次世界大战、大屠杀（系统地屠杀了上百万欧洲的犹太人）以及近5 000万人丧生。

47. **新古典现实主义**：新现实主义与古典现实主义的结合体。其支持者认为，国家的行动可以用结构因素（比如各国军事、经济和政治等实力的分配）和行为主体驱动因素（比如特定领导人的野心）来解释。

48. **新保守主义**：一种强调自由市场资本主义和干预主义外交政策的政治意识形态。主要的新保守主义者包括保罗·沃尔福威茨、唐纳德·拉姆斯菲尔德和约翰·博尔顿。

49. **新自由主义**：一个国际关系的理论学派，认为国家间的合作是可能的，尤其是通过国际组织，因为各国更想要最大化绝对收益，而不是相对其他国家的相对收益。

50. **新现实主义**：一个国际关系的理论学派，认为结构性的制约（比如世界权力分配）而不是人的行为主动性决定了行动者的行为。

51. **诺贝尔和平奖**：每年评选一次，颁给致力于各国实现和平关系的个人或集体。重要的诺贝尔和平奖得主包括亨利·基辛格、马丁·路德·金、纳尔逊·曼德拉、吉米·卡特、贝拉克·奥巴马和马拉拉·尤素福。

52. **进攻性现实主义**：一个理论概念，它假定：国际体系处于无政府状态；大国是全球政治的主要参与者；所有国家都拥有进攻的能力；另一个国家的意图永远无法确定；生存是主要的目标；所有国家都是理性的参与者（即主要关注自身利益）。

53. **排他**：指与设想的身份（在这里指"信奉基督教的西方"）相对的

集体身份（比如"信奉伊斯兰教的伊朗"）的构建过程。在国际关系中经常运用这种方法，一个国家会指出其邻国消极的一面以突出自己的优势。

54. **威斯特伐利亚和约（1648）**：一系列同时在德国奥斯纳布吕克和明斯特签订的和平条约，结束了三十年战争。它帮助巩固了现代世界秩序，在该秩序下，各国平等，国家间的军事冲突要通过建立均势来解决。

55. **现实主义**：一种国际关系的理论学派，他们认为各国是主要的参与者，都有生存的目标并为其安全负责。

56. **现实政治**：一个德语术语，字面意思是"现实的政治"，在国际关系中指决策应该务实而不是以道德或意识形态为考量。

57. **共和党**：美国的右翼政党，成立于1854年；前共和党总统包括乔治·赫伯特·沃克·布什、乔治·W.布什、理查德·尼克松和罗纳德·里根。

58. **保护责任**：国际关系中的一个概念，认为无法保护其公民免受人权侵害的国家会丧失其主权，国际社会相应地享有干预的权利。

59. **国务卿**：美国国务院的首长；美国政府的内阁职位；美国的外长。

60. **什叶派和逊尼派**：伊斯兰教的两个主要分支。公元632年先知穆罕穆德去世后，伊斯兰教分裂成了两个主要派别。伊斯兰的逊尼派是世界宗教中最大的教派。伊斯兰的什叶派是伊斯兰教的第二大教派，占到11%左右，属于少数派。两个教派的差异主要源自其不同的历史经历、政治和社会发展以及民族构成。什叶派不承认前三任逊尼派的哈里发（领导人）是先知的继承人，认为第四任哈里发阿里是先知的真正继承人。

61. **以中国为中心**：一种认为中国是世界中心的意识形态。

62. **主权**：统治特定领土的权利。

63. **苏联（1922—1991）**：苏维埃社会主义共和国联盟，通常简称"苏联"，起源于1917年的俄罗斯十月革命，该革命推翻了俄罗斯帝国的沙皇政权。1922年，在一场与反革命政党的军事冲突中取得胜利后，弗拉基米尔·列宁领导的共产党政权建立了苏联。

64. **超级大国**：这是一个发明于 1944 年的术语，用于描述一个异常强大和富有影响力的国家，通常指冷战期间的美国和苏联，当时两者是世界上最强大的两个国家。

65. **叙利亚内战**（2011 至今）：叙利亚的内部冲突，起初是 2010 年阿拉伯之春的一部分。冲突发生在阿拉维派主导的巴沙尔·阿萨德的阿拉伯复兴社会党叙利亚政府与美国和海湾国家等外国势力支持的多个逊尼派分支派系之间。然而，从 2014 年起，伊斯兰国成为该国最强大的非政府势力。

66. **三十年战争**（1618—1648）：神圣罗马帝国和几个新教德语国家之间的一场冲突，后来升级为几乎波及全欧洲的冲突。

67. **三国协约**：1907 年，英国、俄罗斯帝国和法国一开始为应对德国在欧洲崛起而形成的同盟。该同盟一直持续到第一次世界大战后。

68. **乌克兰战争**（2014 年至今）：乌克兰政府倒台后，俄罗斯吞并克里米亚半岛并占领了乌克兰东部的部分地区，自此该战争爆发。

69. **德意志统一**：中欧最强大的国家普鲁士的国王威廉一世将欧洲中部所有说德语的小国家合并成了一个德意志国家。这大大改变了欧洲的均势。

70. **单边主义**：国际关系中用于描述一个国家采取单独行动的情形。

71. **联合国**：一个成立于 1945 年、由国家组成的国际组织，旨在促进国际和平、安全和合作。

72. **联合国安理会**：联合国的常设机构，旨在维护和平和安全。它有 15 个理事国，其中有 5 个常任理事国（中国、法国、俄罗斯、英国和美国）并拥有否决权。其他理事国由选举产生，任期两年。

73. **《世界人权宣言》**：1948 年联合国通过的一项决议，确定了对基本人权的普世描述。

74. **普世的伊斯兰秩序**：该概念认为伊斯兰教是一种普世宗教，意指其信徒信奉其观点是绝对的，任何不信奉伊斯兰教的人都是异教徒。

75. **越南战争**（1955—1975）：美国和北越的军队之间发生的冷战冲突。1973 年，美国签署了和平条约并从南越撤军，两年后，南越倒台。

76. **反恐战争**：该术语通常指 2001 年 9 月 11 日世贸中心遭到袭击后，美国主导在中东各地打击基地组织等非国家"恐怖分子"组织的行动。巴基斯坦的无人机轰炸、占领阿富汗以及其他秘密和公开的行动都属于这一行动。

77. **大规模杀伤性武器**：该术语指能够轻而易举杀死大批人的武器。通常指生化武器或者核武器。

78. **魏玛共和国**：该立宪国家成立于德国在第一次世界大战中战败后，一直持续到 1933 年阿道夫·希特勒上台。

79. **威斯特伐利亚体系**：自从 1648 年同时在德国奥斯纳布吕克和明斯特签订和平条约结束三十年战争后，该秩序管理了欧洲的国际关系。根据协议，各国平等，国家间的军事冲突要通过建立均势解决。该体系以主权、合法性和均势的概念为前提，在殖民期间强加给了世界其他国家。

80. **世界银行**：一个国际金融组织，设立于第二次世界大战后，最初是为了资助欧洲重建。如今，它旨在帮助发展中国家获取研发项目和减少贫困的贷款。

81. **世界秩序**：大体而言是指管理国际关系的稳定体系，建立在对国家力量的义务和限制等共识的基础之上。

82. **第一次世界大战**（1914—1918）：同盟国（德国、奥地利-匈牙利和奥斯曼帝国）与获胜的协约国（英国、法国、俄罗斯以及 1917 后的美国）之间的全球性冲突。1 600 多万人在该战争中丧生。

83. **第二次世界大战**（1939—1945）：轴心国（德国、意大利和日本）和获胜的同盟国（英国及其殖民国、法国、苏联和美国）之间的全球性冲突。

84. **世界自然基金会**：一个旨在促进生物多样性、保护以及限制人类对地球环境造成影响的非政府组织。

人名表

1. 亚里士多德(公元前384—公元前322年),希腊哲学家。与他的老师柏拉图一样,亚里士多德是西方哲学的重要鼻祖之一。亚里士多德现存的大部分作品,比如《尼各马可伦理学》和《形而上学》,都是为其吕克昂学院的教育而著的。

2. 巴沙尔·阿萨德(1965年生),2000年起担任叙利亚的总统。他是哈菲兹·阿萨德的次子,起初是眼科医生,但1994年其兄长意外死亡后,他被任命为其总统父亲的继承人。

3. 约翰·博尔顿(1948年生),新保守派的政治评论员和外交家,2005年8月至2006年12月期间担任美国驻联合国大使。

4. 拿破仑·波拿巴(1769—1821),18世纪90年代法国大革命期间最年轻又最成功的将军之一。1804年,他宣布自己为法国的皇帝,经过一系列重大胜利后,使法国控制了欧洲大陆的大片领土。1815年,他在滑铁卢之战中败北,被流放至南大西洋的圣赫勒拿岛。

5. 斯蒂芬·布鲁克斯,达特茅斯学院的政府学副教授。他以与威廉·沃尔福思合作闻名,著有《创造安全:跨国公司、全球化和不断变化的冲突算法》。

6. 乔治·赫伯特·沃克·布什(1924年生),美国的第41任总统,罗纳德·里根的副总统,曾任中情局局长,是一位外交家。

7. 乔治·W.布什(1946年生),美国的第43任总统。他服务了两个任期,任期为2001年至2009年。

8. 吉米·卡特(1924年生),美国的第39任总统。他以应对伊朗革命闻名。

9. 卡斯尔雷勋爵,爱尔兰和英国的政治家和外长。他因1814年至1815年期间代表英国出席维也纳会议而被人铭记。

10. 比尔·克林顿(1946年生),美国的第42任总统,于1993年至2001

年期间执政。

11. **希拉里·克林顿**（1947年生），美国的政治家和外交家。她于2009年至2013年任国务卿，是2016年总统大选的候选人。

12. **德怀特·戴维·艾森豪威尔**（1890—1969），美国的第34任总统，第二次世界大战期间的联军总司令。

13. **威廉·扬德尔·埃利奥特**（1896—1979），杰出的美国历史学家，第二次世界大战后担任美国国家安全委员会的委员，曾为六位总统建言献策。他是亨利·基辛格在哈佛大学的导师。

14. **杰拉尔德·福特**（1913—2006），美国的第38任总统。1973年，丑闻迫使其前任斯皮罗·阿格纽辞职后，他当选为理查德·尼克松总统的副总统，此前他是众议院的议员。1974年8月，尼克松辞职后，他成为总统。

15. **弗朗西斯·福山**（1952年生），美国的政治学家、政治经济学家和作家。

16. **阿道夫·希特勒**（1889—1945），纳粹党的领袖，1933年至1945年间德国的独裁者。他的扩张政策引发了第二次世界大战。

17. **萨缪尔·菲利普斯·亨廷顿**（1927—2008），哈佛大学的国际关系学教授。他的著作《文明的冲突与世界秩序的重建》被普遍认为是分析冷战后国际秩序最有影响力的作品。

18. **沃尔夫冈·伊申格尔**（1946年生），德国外长，2001年至2006年任德国驻美国大使。

19. **罗伯特·卡根**（1958年生），美国的新保守派政治评论员，曾担任希拉里·克林顿、约翰·克里和约翰·麦凯恩的顾问。

20. **伊曼努尔·康德**（1724—1804），普鲁士（今为现代德国）哲学家，致力于为"所有人都值得平等对待和尊重"的思想辩护，该思想的基础是"只有认为自己的准则是普遍规律，才能采取行动"（即"绝对命令"）。

21. 保罗·肯尼迪（1945 年生），生于英国的耶鲁大学历史教授，以其国际关系著作闻名。他最著名的作品为《大国的兴衰》(1987)。

22. 罗伯特·基欧汉（1941 年生），美国普林斯顿大学的政治学教授。他与新自由派的机构主义——基于国际机构可以促进国家间合作的观点——紧密联系，另外值得关注的是，他与小约瑟夫·奈合著了《权力与互相依存》。

23. 弗里茨·克雷默（1908—2003），出生于德国的美国军事顾问，他说服了好友亨利·基辛格继续深造。

24. 尼科洛·马基雅维利（1469—1527），意大利的哲学家和外交家，以其所著的《君主论》闻名于世。在书中，他认为，为了获得权力，有时使用武力和做出不道德的行为是必不可少的；这也是情有可原的，因为为了达到这个目的必须采用一切手段。

25. 约翰·米尔斯海默（1947 年生），芝加哥大学的国际关系学教授。他 2001 年的作品《大国政治的悲剧》使他成为新现实主义政治学派最重要的国际关系理论家。该作品介绍了进攻性现实主义的理论。

26. 克莱门斯·文策尔·冯·梅特涅（1773—1859），奥地利的贵族、外交家，在 1821 年至 1848 年间担任首相。他在举办维也纳会议中发挥了重要作用，该会议建立了欧洲新秩序。

27. 汉斯·摩根索（1904—1980），德国的政治理论家，主要在美国工作。他被认为是最杰出的古典现实主义者。

28. 先知穆罕默德（570—632），伊斯兰教的创始人。610 年起，他经历了一系列预见的事件，这些经历后来被转录为伊斯兰教的圣书《古兰经》，它是伊斯兰教教义和教法的基础。

29. 瓦利·纳斯尔（1960 年生），美国的政治学家，专攻中东的国际关系。他目前担任约翰斯·霍普金斯大学高级国际学院的院长。

30. 理查德·尼克松（1913—1994），美国的第 37 任总统，是第一位辞职的美国总统，因为他卷入了水门事件。

31. 小约瑟夫·奈（1937 年生），哈佛大学的美国政治学教授。他与罗

伯特·基欧汉合著了《权力与互相依存》（1977），有效地构建了新自由派的机构主义。

32. 贝拉克·奥巴马（1961 年生），美国的第 44 任总统，2008 年当选。他是美国的第一位黑人总统。

33. 巴麦尊勋爵（1784—1865），在 1855 年至 1858 年和 1859 年至 1865 年期间担任英国首相。

34. 奥波德·冯·兰克（1795—1886），德国历史学家，创建了基于档案研究的历史叙事法。

35. 纳尔逊·洛克菲勒（1908—1979），美国的第 41 任副总统，第 49 任纽约州州长，杰出的美国商人和慈善家；他来自富裕的洛克菲勒家族。

36. 西奥多·罗斯福（1858—1919），美国的第 26 任总统。他以与现实主义思想学派紧密相连著称。

37. 安妮-玛丽·斯劳特（1958 年生），普林斯顿大学的政治和国际事务教授，外交政策分析师，现任新美国基金会主席。

38. 巴鲁赫·德·斯宾诺莎（1632—1677），理性主义传统的犹太裔荷兰哲学家。他的主要作品包括《逻辑政治论》和《伦理学》。

39. 约瑟夫·斯大林（1878—1953），1924 年至 1953 年期间担任苏联领导人。

40. 修昔底德（公元前 460—公元前 395 年），希腊历史学家，以记载公元前 431—404 年雅典和斯巴达之间战争的《伯罗奔尼撒战争史》而闻名于世。他被认为是"现实政治"的第一批支持者之一。现实政治认为在政治中，权力和利益应该置于思想和道德之上。

41. 詹姆斯·特拉布（1954 年生），专注国际事务的美国记者，是《纽约时报》的撰稿人。

42. 斯蒂芬·沃尔特（1955 年生），哈佛大学的国际关系学教授，新现实主义政治思想学派的国际关系理论家。他提出了称为"威胁均衡"的理论概念。

43. **伍德罗·威尔逊**（1856—1924），美国的第 28 任总统，任期为 1913 年至 1921 年。他因其自由的理想主义原则和在一战后试图借助民主原则重建欧洲中发挥的作用而闻名。

44. **威廉·沃尔福思**（1959 年生），达特茅斯学院的美国政府学教授。他以与斯蒂芬·布鲁克斯的合作及其作品《难以解释的平衡：冷战时期的权力与认知》而闻名。

45. **保罗·沃尔福威茨**（1943 年生），新保守派学者、世界银行前总裁，乔治·W. 布什执政期间的副国防部长。他在发动伊拉克战争中发挥了重要作用，这场战争最后黯然收场。

46. **法里德·扎卡利亚**（1964 年生），印度裔美国记者、作家和新现实主义学者。他是美国《外交》杂志的主编、《时代周刊》的总主编，特别值得一提的是，还是《后美国世界》一书的作者。

WAYS IN TO THE TEXT

KEY POINTS

- Henry Kissinger (b. 1923) is a German-born American scholar, diplomat, and Nobel Peace Prize-winning* statesman.

- His book *World Order* (2014) offers a historical account of how what he terms "world order"*—a stable system of relations between states—has been understood in different parts of the world.

- The book examines the continuing debate, heightened since the fall of the Soviet Union* in 1991, between "realists,"* who contend that the risk of instability and conflict remains high, and "liberal internationalists,"* who believe that cooperation between nations will grow if policies that promote international structures fostering a liberal* world order are pursued.

Who Is Henry Kissinger?

Heinz Alfred "Henry" Kissinger is one of the best-known and most controversial statesmen of the twentieth century. He was United States national security advisor* (1969–75) and secretary of state* (1973–77) during the presidencies of Richard Nixon* and Gerald Ford.*¹ During this time, he was accused of being complicit in human rights violations.

Kissinger was born in 1923 in the Bavarian town of Fürth in southern Germany.² His family was prosperous and Jewish. With the rise of the Nazis* in 1933, and the persecution of Germany's Jews that Nazism brought with it, his family were increasingly threatened. In 1938 the Kissinger family fled for America, as did many German Jews. There Kissinger adopted "Henry," the anglicized version of his name, although he continued to speak with a heavy German accent. After the United States joined World War II* in 1941, Kissinger was drafted into the US army and became a naturalized American citizen. His fluent German and knowledge of Nazi Germany* saw him work in counterintelligence (efforts to prevent spying), at which he excelled.

After the war, Kissinger enrolled at Harvard University, where he studied politics and philosophy. He earned his Bachelor of Arts in 1950, his Master of Arts in 1951, and his Doctor of Philosophy in 1954. Kissinger was awarded a faculty position at Harvard, emerging as a vocal critic of American foreign policy. This brought him to the attention of senior members of the right-wing Republican Party* such as presidential candidate Nelson Rockefeller.* In 1969, President Richard Nixon asked Kissinger to serve as his national security advisor; for the next five years they would work to reshape the realm of international politics.

Kissinger's skilled diplomacy earned him the Nobel Peace Prize for his role in bringing about the American withdrawal from the Vietnam War* in 1973—a brutal Cold War* proxy war (that is, a war begun by two major powers that do not participate in the conflict) fought between American-backed South Vietnamese forces and the communist North Vietnamese forces backed by the Soviet Union and China. Since leaving public office in 1977, Kissinger has continued to advise successive US governments on foreign policy.

What Does *World Order* Say?

World Order: Reflections on the Character of Nations and the

Course of History offers an analysis of the history of one of the more challenging questions facing humanity: What is "world order"—roughly, a stable system of international relations—and how can we bring about a universally acceptable form of this international system?

To answer this question, Kissinger analyzes four principal forms of world order:

- The European "Westphalian" system,* founded on notions of sovereignty* (the right to govern a specific territory), legitimacy* (lawfulness), balance of power* (balance of military and political power between the states that constitute the international order), and national interests* (things a nation believes are vital to its political, military, economic, or diplomatic reputation and comfort, or to its survival).
- The universalist Islamic order* (an order founded on notions of the supremacy of the Islamic faith)
- The Sino-centric* Chinese order (according to which China is at the center of the civilized world)
- The American order, which is premised on the concepts of freedom, justice, and representative democracy.

He also addresses the three secondary conceptions of world order that developed in Japan, India, and Persia (modern-day Iran). As Kissinger points out, the Japanese and Indian conceptions of world orders developed separately from the Chinese order, largely due to their geographic isolation from China—Japan is an island nation and India is separated from China by the Himalayan mountain range. Similarly, the Persian conception of world order developed separately due to its geographic position at the crossroads of several civilizations: the Asian, European, Indian, and Islamic. Even though Persia adopted Islam as a national religion, its ancient heritage and its decision to subscribe to a minority sect of Islam—Shi'ism*—left it with a distinctly different conception of world order.

Today, the dominant conception of world order is the Westphalian system that developed in the seventeenth century after the brutalities of the Thirty Years' War* (a European conflict between the political body known as the Holy Roman Empire* and several Germanic states that escalated into most of Europe). At the end of the war, with much of continental Europe suffering the consequences of a serious conflict, European statesmen developed the concepts of sovereignty, legitimacy, balance of power, and national interests as a means of resolving future differences. On the signing of the treaty known as the Peace of Westphalia* in 1648, which brought an end to the war, the signatories agreed to respect the legitimacy of the leaders of each state and not to interfere with their internal affairs. They established diplomatic representatives in each other's countries to resolve disputes peacefully. More importantly, in the event that one state became too powerful, it was agreed in principle that the others would form an alliance to restore equilibrium in the system, which came to be known as a "balance of power."

After centuries of evolution and inevitable modification, the Westphalian system still generally serves as the scaffolding for modern international relations. However, as Kissinger shows in

World Order, it is no longer universally and easily accepted; the current international system can be understood as being a relic of the colonial* era—that is, a system forced on colonial subjects by European "masters." Today, challenges come from the alternative conceptions of world order, whether the Chinese, the Islamic, or the American.

For example, the Chinese system, being Sino-centric, views China as the center of the world and, as an emerging superpower, China will inevitably want to increasingly impose itself on the wider world. According to the universalist Islamic conception of world order, those who subscribe to Islam are part of the *dar al-Islam**—the "house of Islam"; those who do not subscribe to Islam belong to *dar al-harb*,* the "realm of war," and are cast as outsiders, "others,"* who need either to be converted or face the wrath of God. The most extreme version of this conception is preached by militant groups such as the Islamic State of Iraq and Syria (ISIS),* its allies in al-Qaeda,* and its Nigerian affiliate, Boko Haram.*

Why Does *World Order* Matter?

World Order is a significant contribution to an ongoing debate among scholars of American foreign policy and of international relations about how a new world order can be forged. The debate is very largely a product of the end of the Cold War of 1947–91. Apart from the military threat it presented, the Cold War was an ideological standoff between the two most obvious beneficiaries of World War II, the United States and the Soviet Union. While both emerged as superpowers* after 1945, they were entirely opposed ideologically.

Both wanted to impose their ideologies on the world. The Soviet Union was a communist power (that is, property was held in common ownership and labor organized for common benefit). The United States, which saw itself as the leader of what was called the "free world" (denoting the non-communist countries of the world) stood for capitalism* (an economic system in which industry and trade are held in private hands) and democracy. It would seem that American values prevailed when, essentially bankrupt, the Soviet Union collapsed in 1991. Yet the Cold War had provided a certain degree of stability to the Eastern Bloc;* the inevitable question after 1991 was what, if anything, could replace it.

In the United States, which then emerged as the sole superpower, scholars were divided into two main groups. "Realists," such as the international relations scholars John Mearsheimer* and Stephen Walt,* believed that very little would change with the collapse of the Soviet Union because the nature of international politics had not been fundamentally altered: states would continue to operate on the basis of how they could best exercise their own power, assessing and reacting to events in terms of their national interests. According to this analysis, it was unlikely that the rate of interstate conflict would decrease.

The second group, "liberal internationalists," such as the international relations scholars Anne-Marie Slaughter,* Robert Keohane,* and Joseph Nye, Jr.,* believed that the post-Cold War era would usher in a new age of international cooperation and that the power politics of the great powers (Great Britain, France, Germany, Russia, China, and the United States) would be consigned to the past. This group was more optimistic, believing that interstate conflict would be reduced if international bodies such as the United Nations* were strengthened. It was not a view that necessarily argued against military intervention, for example if intervention was used in instances where governments were unable—or unwilling—to protect their citizens.

Even though Kissinger declares himself a realist, the views expressed in *World Order* suggest that he tends to straddle these two positions. On the one hand, his outlook is realist in that he believes that the projection of power and securing legitimacy— roughly, a legal basis to exist—are central to the conduct of foreign relations, and that foreign interventions should be decided on the basis of a nation's national interests rather than by theoretical notions of morality. On the other, he also holds the liberal position that international institutions need to be strengthened in order to facilitate cooperation and prevent conflict.

---

1. Christopher Hitchens, *The Trial of Henry Kissinger* (London: Verso, 2001).
2. Robert Dallek, *Nixon and Kissinger: Partners in Power* (London: HarperCollins, 2007), 34.

SECTION 1
INFLUENCES

MODULE 1
THE AUTHOR AND THE HISTORICAL CONTEXT

KEY POINTS

- *World Order* is a significant contribution to the long-standing debate about how to create a new world order.*
- Henry Kissinger is a Nobel Prize-winning* diplomat, scholar, and statesman of international stature. He served as US secretary of state*—the highest diplomatic position in the US government—between 1973 and 1977.
- The inability to bring about a stable world order following the end of the Cold War* (a decades-long nuclear standoff between the Soviet Union* and the United States, and nations aligned to each, which ended with the collapse of the Soviet Union in 1991) convinced Kissinger that writing this book was necessary.

Why Read This Text?

Henry Kissinger's *World Order: Reflections on the Character of Nations and the Course of History* provides an important analysis of one of the greatest challenges mankind has faced: how to bring about a universally accepted world order—a structure of international relations, balances of power, and governance on which citizens of all nations can agree. One of the Western world's most respected statesmen and foreign-policy analysts, Kissinger is uniquely positioned to examine this key question. He shows that there are currently four major conceptualizations of world order:

- The European Westphalian* system
- The universal Islamic order*

- The Chinese Sino-centric order*
- The American order.

Of these, the dominant system today is the Westphalian system first developed in the seventeenth century, if subsequently much changed—an order founded on notions of sovereignty,* legitimacy,* balance of power,* and national interests.* But as Kissinger makes plain in *World Order*, it is a system under attack from all directions. The path toward a viable new world order remains uncertain.

For those interested in the concept of world order, or in international politics more generally, *World Order* offers a comprehensive overview of world history and provides insights into the historical development of key sources of conflict and stability. This is particularly important today, now that the challenges that typically confronted states during the twentieth century—not just wars, but the Cold War too—are significantly altered. New threats have emerged from entities that are not states themselves in any conventional sense, most obviously the militant religious group known as the Islamic State of Iraq and Syria* (ISIS). Nature, likewise, presents its own threats in the form of potentially devastating pandemics, such as the outbreak of the infectious disease Ebola* that killed almost 25,000 people in West Africa in 2014.[1] As the challenges facing states become increasingly global, a new world order is needed ever more urgently.[2]

> "If I had to choose between justice and disorder, on the one hand, and injustice and order, on the other, I would always choose the latter."
>
> —— Henry Kissinger, in Robert Dallek, *Nixon and Kissinger*

Author's Life

Heinz Alfred Kissinger was born on May 27, 1923 in the small Bavarian town of Fürth, in what was known as Weimar* Germany, the fragile republic set up in the disastrous aftermath of World War I.* His family was middle-class and Jewish; his mother, Paula Stern, came from a well-to-do family, and his father, Louis, was a schoolmaster at a state school. The Kissingers enjoyed considerable status in the town. Heinz Kissinger has a younger brother, Walter.[3]

Kissinger's adolescent years were increasingly difficult. The rise to power of Adolf Hitler* and the Nazi Party* he led in 1933 made Germany not merely an unpleasant but an actively dangerous place for an intellectually curious young Jewish boy.[4] In August 1938, Heinz and his family fled from Germany to America, where they had relatives. Though he shed his German name "Heinz" in favor of "Henry," his obvious German accent remained.

In 1943, Kissinger joined the army to fight in World War II.* He was sent to France, then to Germany, where he played an active role in the denazification of Germany after the end of the war in 1945. It was here that he found his first calling. His intelligence, fluent German, and firsthand knowledge of Nazi Germany made him an obvious asset.

After the war, Kissinger enrolled at Harvard, studying 16 hours a day and earning the highest honors. It was at Harvard, in 1949, that he married Ann Fleischer. They had two children, eventually divorcing in 1964. After his BA degree, Kissinger went on to earn his MA in 1951 and his PhD in 1954.

Having secured a tenured position at Harvard, Kissinger published a scathing series of articles attacking US foreign policy that caught the attention of the businessman Nelson Rockefeller,* then a presidential candidate, who enrolled Kissinger in his campaign as an advisor. After Rockefeller failed to win the Republican* nomination for the 1968 election, Richard Nixon,* who won the nomination (and the election), hired Kissinger as his national security advisor.* In 1973, Nixon appointed him secretary of state. Since leaving public life in 1977, Kissinger has remained a central figure in debates about the conduct of US foreign policy.

Author's Background

The Cold War had a profound impact on Kissinger's intellectual life. This ideological and geostrategic* conflict between the United States and Soviet Union began just as he started his education at Harvard (in a geostrategic conflict, politics and international relations are influenced by geography and by military and political strategy). Always alert to the past, Kissinger's PhD thesis "Peace, Legitimacy, and the Equilibrium (A Study of the Statesmanship of Castlereagh* and Metternich*)" focused on the role of statesmen in the Congress of Vienna,* the convention that forged a new European order after the defeat of Napoleon Bonaparte* in 1815.

Between 1955 and 1961, Kissinger published a dozen articles that criticized the conventional wisdom of foreign-policy making, garnering him national attention as a leading foreign-policy critic. In 1955, he published an article in the journal *Foreign Affairs* that attacked the administration of President Eisenhower* for pursuing a policy of massive nuclear retaliation—or mutually assured destruction*—in order to avoid war with the Soviet Union, and he advocated a strategy of fighting limited wars* to counter the expansion of the Soviet Union's influence. When this article was published in book form as *Nuclear Weapons and Foreign Policy* in 1957, it was an instant bestseller and Kissinger became a household name.

Today, Kissinger is best known for his role in the administration of President Nixon, who was forced to resign after disgracing himself in a political scandal, and his successor Gerald Ford.* In this time, Kissinger put his knowledge of foreign policy into practice, which led to an unmatched series of foreign-policy successes. In an 18-month period during 1972–3, Kissinger helped bring about "the end of the Vietnam War,* an opening to China, a summit with the Soviet Union even while escalating the military effort in response to a North Vietnamese offensive, the switch of Egypt from a Soviet ally to close cooperation with the United States, two disengagement agreements in the Middle East ... and the start of the European Security Conference, whose outcome over the long term severely weakened Soviet control of Eastern Europe."[5]

---

1. Centers for Disease Control and Prevention, "2014 Ebola Outbreak in West Africa–Case Counts," accessed November 18, 2015, http://www.cdc.gov/ vhf/ebola/outbreaks/2014-west-africa/case-counts.html.
2. Wolfgang Ischinger, "The World According to Kissinger: How to Defend Global Order," *Foreign Affairs* (March/April 2015), accessed October 1, 2015, https://www.foreignaffairs.com/reviews/2015-03-01/world-according-kissinger.
3. Robert Dallek, *Nixon and Kissinger* (London: HarperCollins, 2007), 34.
4. Dallek, *Nixon and Kissinger*, 34.
5. Henry Kissinger, *World Order* (New York: Penguin, 2015), 307–8.

MODULE 2
ACADEMIC CONTEXT

KEY POINTS

- *World Order* is relevant to two fields of study: diplomatic history, which focuses on the history of diplomatic relations, and international relations, which focuses on relations between states and nongovernmental organizations.
- Theories of international relations are broken down into two camps: realist* and liberal internationalist.* Realists believe that states resort to aggression when their national interests are threatened, and that conflict is a constant of international politics. Liberals believe that in the absence of a dominant power (known as a hegemon),* states will tend to cooperate and that such cooperation is the norm of international politics.
- Henry Kissinger is a realist, a point made plain by the way he conducted foreign relations during his time at the White House.

The Work in Its Context

Henry Kissinger's *World Order: Reflections on the Character of Nations and the Course of History* fits within two closely related academic disciplines: diplomatic history and international relations. While Kissinger is a famed practitioner of foreign policy, he is actually a diplomatic historian by trade, whose research focused on the conduct of foreign relations.

Diplomatic historians use techniques such as archival research, memoirs, oral history, and document analysis, to develop a historical understanding of relations between states. Today, as governments make an increasing number of documents available to researchers, it is a field that has grown in popularity, both as an academic discipline and commercially, with major publishers putting out hugely successful works that deal with diplomacy. Kissinger's *World Order* is a prime example.

International relations is more a subdiscipline of politics. Its primary focus is the way in which countries and nongovernmental bodies, such as international organizations like the World Bank* (an organization founded to make loans to developing countries in return for economic reform), corporations (Microsoft, Apple, and Gap, for example), or terrorist groups (today, most obviously the Islamic State of Iraq and Syria),* interact with each other.

This field is by no means new. Scholars and philosophers, among them the Greek philosopher Aristotle,* the ancient Greek historian Thucydides,* and the fifteenth- and sixteenth-century political theorist Niccolò Machiavelli,* have long been interested in how groups of people (or nations) interact, and have developed sophisticated theories to help explain this. Such theories, like realism or idealism,* can play a major role in influencing how foreign-policy practitioners operate and what informs their decisions.

> "I want you to meet this fellow Henry Kissinger, who is a combination of [Immanuel] Kant and [Benedict de] Spinoza."
> ——William Y. Elliott, in Robert Dallek, *Nixon and Kissinger*

Overview of the Field

As a work of diplomatic history, Kissinger's *World Order* draws on the intellectual heritage of the nineteenth-century German historian

Leopold von Ranke,* considered the father of the field. Ranke argued that only through archival research and the analysis of historical documents can any kind of objective truth—an accurate picture of historical events—be reached. For Ranke, historical events were best understood when developed into a chronological narrative, this being the optimum way to show the relationship between cause and effect. Both of these techniques are evident not just in *World Order* but in Kissinger's earlier historical works and in his memoirs, for which he often used documents produced during his time at the White House.

Kissinger's work also plays into a central debate among scholars of international relations, who are historically divided into two main factions: realists and idealists. Realists, such as Kissinger and presidents Theodore Roosevelt* and Richard Nixon,* see international politics as a matter of sovereign nations (a sovereign nation being an independent state that governs itself) balancing each other's power.* All three also believed in the projection of American power. As the international relations scholar Joseph Nye, Jr.* points out, to realists, "world order* is the product of a stable distribution of power among the major states."[1] Kissinger's association with realism stems from his time at Harvard, where Hans Morgenthau*—a classical realist*—convinced him that global politics was defined by power and a dispassionate calculation of a state's interests.[2]

The second school of thought is that of idealism (or liberalism). In American terms, it is associated primarily with President Woodrow Wilson,* president of the US between 1913 and 1921, and President Jimmy Carter,* in office between 1977 and 1981. Idealism bases its analysis on the assumption that nations and people are inherently good, and promotes values such as democracy and human rights. For idealist thinkers, cooperation among states should be encouraged, especially through international organizations such as the United Nations.*

Academic Influences

As a young scholar, two figures had a direct influence on Kissinger's intellectual growth and later career. The first was Fritz Kraemer,* a fellow German émigré and academic, whom Kissinger had met after joining the US army. According to Kissinger's biographer, "Kraemer helped arrange jobs for Henry that strengthened his self-confidence and added to feelings that he was not just a naturalized American but a German and ... a European with a keen feel for international affairs."[3] More importantly, it was Kraemer who convinced Kissinger to use the GI Bill* (legislation passed to provide benefits to former servicemen) to enroll at Harvard and to apply for a New York state scholarship.[4]

While at Harvard, Kissinger met his second principal influence, the historian William Y. Elliott,* a notable scholar of governance who had served as a presidential advisor for six US presidents and who agreed to serve as Kissinger's mentor. Elliott encouraged Kissinger's appetite for knowledge, demanding, for example, that he read 25 books on Immanuel Kant* and write a review of his works. Determined to impress, Kissinger completed the assignment in just three months, prompting Elliott to describe to his colleagues that he had "not had any students in the past five years ... who have had the depth and philosophical insight shown by Mr. Kissinger," whom he described as "a combination of Kant and [the famed Dutch philosopher] Spinoza."*5 Through Elliott's encouragement, guidance, and support, Kissinger applied for and was accepted into Harvard's PhD program.

---

1. Joseph S. Nye, Jr., "What New World Order?" *Foreign Affairs* (Spring 1992): 84–5, accessed December 7, 2015, https://www.foreignaffairs.com/articles/1992-03-01/what-new-world-order.
2. Hans Morgenthau, *Politics Among Nations: The Struggle for Power and Peace* (New York: Knopf, 1948).
3. Robert Dallek, *Nixon and Kissinger* (London: HarperCollins, 2007), 37–8.
4. Dallek, *Nixon and Kissinger*, 39.
5. Dallek, *Nixon and Kissinger*, 41.

MODULE 3
THE PROBLEM

KEY POINTS

- When *World Order* was published in 2014, the debate about the nature of world order* had subsided since a flurry of activity in the 1990s and early 2000s.
- In the 1990s, the realist* school of international relations contended that the new world order would be based on the projection of Western values of individualism and liberty, and the belief that disorder will probably exist on the fault lines of the world's major civilizations. For the liberal* school of international relations, a new world order could be achieved through the strengthening and reform of international institutions such as the United Nations.*
- *World Order* tends to straddle these debates, drawing on both realist and liberal views.

Core Question

The central question of Henry Kissinger's *World Order* is: What is world order and how is it viewed around the world? The idea of a new world order is not particularly new—and nor is it unique to Kissinger's work, directly reflecting a debate among scholars of international relations since the end of the Cold War* (particularly with respect to American foreign policy). After the end of the Soviet Union* in 1991, the term became closely associated with the administration of President George H. W. Bush,* which declared its intention to renounce the unilateralism* (action taken by a single state without the agreement or support of other states) of the Cold

War era in favor of multilateral* diplomacy and, if necessary, military action.

Following the collapse of the Berlin Wall*, the US political scientist Francis Fukuyama* sparked a contentious debate over the question of what a post-Cold War order would look like with his 1989 article "The End of History?," subsequently published as the book *The End of History and the Last Man* in 1992. Fukuyama believed that a new order would develop based on Western liberal and democratic traditions. Over the course of the next 25 years, numerous scholars of international relations have contributed to this debate. That said, no consensus emerged as to what shape the post-Cold War order might take, nor on what role the United States would have in shaping it.

> "This book grew out of a dinner conversation with Charles Hill ... a valued member of the [state department's] policy planning staff when I served as secretary of state a lifetime ago ... At the dinner, we concluded that the crisis in the concept of world order was the ultimate problem of our day."
>
> ——Henry Kissinger, *World Order: Reflections on the Character of Nations and the Course of History*

The Participants

After the publication of Fukuyama's *The End of History and the Last Man*, several scholars developed competing views on what the post-Cold War order would look like. In 1992, the international relations scholar Joseph Nye, Jr.* published a response to

Fukuyama in an article in the journal *Foreign Affairs* that asked "What New World Order?" For him, "rather than the end of history, the post-Cold War world is witnessing a return of history in the diversity of sources of international conflict."[1] The next year, the US political scientist Samuel P. Huntington* published a detailed response to Fukuyama in the article "The Clash of Civilizations?" and the subsequent book *The Clash of Civilizations and the Remaking of World Order* (1996). Huntington argued that "in the emerging [post-Cold War] world, Western belief in the universality of Western culture suffers three problems: it is false; it is immoral; and it is dangerous."[2] For Huntington, "the fundamental source of conflict in this new world will not be primarily ideological or primarily economic. The great divisions among humankind and the dominating source of conflict will be cultural. Nation states will remain the most powerful actors in world affairs, but the principal conflicts of global politics will occur between nations and groups of different civilizations."[3]

The Contemporary Debate

Fukuyama and Huntington's theses prompted a response from liberal international relations scholars, who believed that a just new world order depended on the strengthening of international institutions. In 1997, the international relations scholar Anne-Marie Slaughter* published the article "The Real New World Order," in which she argued that a new world order was emerging, but not in the form of supra-state (above-state) bodies such as the United Nations* or the World Bank,* as Kissinger would argue.

Instead, Slaughter believed that this new world order was actually emerging at the sub-state (below-state) level where a complex and interconnected network of representatives from bodies such as courts, regulatory agencies, and nongovernmental bodies such as the World Wildlife Fund* and Greenpeace,* cooperate to deal with transnational issues such as crime, terrorism, environmental degradation, and international relations—a process she called "transgovernmentalism."[4] This process is driven by incredible advances in technology, above all the Internet.

In 2001, the professor of international relations John Mearsheimer* entered the debate about the post-Cold War world order in his book *The Tragedy of Great Power Politics*. In it, Mearsheimer developed his concept of offensive realism.* This holds that the international system is anarchical* (that is, ungoverned), the great powers are the main actors in global politics, all states possess offensive capabilities, states can never be certain of each other's intentions, survival is the primary objective, and all states are rational actors (that is, they act according to rational decisions). In short, Mearsheimer believed that the end of the Cold War did not reduce the likelihood of continued rivalry between the most powerful nations.[5]

In the aftermath of the terrorist attacks on the United States on September 11, 2001 (9/11)* and the subsequent War on Terror* (that is, American-led actions throughout the Middle East against non-state organizations and the US-led wars in Afghanistan* and Iraq),* the debate about a new world order floundered. However, in the mid-2000s there was an intellectual backlash against the unilateralism of the George W. Bush* administration (that is, its propensity to act alone) and its efforts to use American leverage in international institutions to promote its own narrow vision of a US-led world order.[6] In particular, liberals were dismayed by the appointment of two key architects of the failed Iraq War, John Bolton* and Paul Wolfowitz* as, respectively, the US ambassador to the United Nations and the president of the World Bank.

In response, in his book *The Parliament of Man: The Past, Present, and Future of the United Nations* (2006), Paul Kennedy* called for the strengthening of international institutions, especially the United Nations. Similarly, in 2009 the scholars of government Stephen Brooks* and William Wohlforth* argued that there were five steps that the new administration of President Barack Obama* needed to take to reform international institutions and to forge a new order:

- Play up the reciprocal benefits of proposed reforms
- Ensure the revised framework provides public benefits, such as stifling terrorism and stabilizing the global economy
- Link the proposed order to the current order
- Consider possible objections from other states and then act so as to minimize their legal force
- Persuade others that change is needed.[7]

---

1. Joseph S. Nye, Jr., "What New World Order?" *Foreign Affairs* (Spring 1992): 84–5, accessed December 7, 2015, https://www.foreignaffairs.com/articles/1992-03-01/what-new-world-order.
2. Samuel P. Huntington, *The Clash of Civilizations and the Remaking of World Order* (London: Simon and Schuster, 2002), 310.

3. Samuel P. Huntington, "The Clash of Civilizations?" *Foreign Affairs* (Summer 1993): 22, accessed December 7, 2015, https://www.foreignaffairs.com/articles/united-states/1993-06-01/clash-civilizations.
4. Anne-Marie Slaughter, "The Real New World Order," *Foreign Affairs* (September/October 1997): 183–4, accessed December 7, 2015, https://www.foreignaffairs.com/articles/1997-09-01/real-new-world-order.
5. John J. Mearsheimer, *The Tragedy of Great Power Politics* (New York: W. W. Norton, 2001).
6. Daniel W. Drezner, "The New New World Order," *Foreign Affairs* (March/April 2007): 34–46, accessed December 7, 2015, https://www.foreignaffairs. com/articles/2007-03-01/new-new-world-order.
7. Stephen G. Brooks and William C. Wohlforth, "Reshaping the World Order," *Foreign Affairs* (March/April 2009): 59, accessed December 7, 2015, https://www.foreignaffairs.com/articles/2009-03-01/reshaping-world-order.

MODULE 4
THE AUTHOR'S CONTRIBUTION

KEY POINTS

- Henry Kissinger does not specifically state how to bring about a new world order.*
- He examines the different understandings of world order in different parts of the globe and how these evolved over time.
- Building on the ongoing debate between the realist* and the liberal* schools of international relations, Kissinger uses European, Islamic, Asian, and American history to show how each of these civilizations understands the concept of world order.

Author's Aims

Henry Kissinger's primary objective when writing *World Order* was to explain the various interpretations of the concept of world order, to explain how these developed, and to identify potential obstacles to achieving a universally accepted world order in the future. For him, the central problem is that "no truly global 'world order' has ever existed";[1] until comparatively recently, communication between the regions of the world was limited at best. As a result, different views about world order developed in different regions and in different civilizations: the European Westphalian* order, with its principles of sovereignty* and legitimacy;* the Islamic order,* founded on the notion of the supremacy of the Muslim faith;* the Sino-centric* Asian order, according to which China should automatically be considered the center of any world order; and the American order, informed by the principles of democracy and liberty; and two secondary Asian ones—the Japanese and Indian—which developed due to their relative geographic isolation from China.

Today, however, civilizations that had previously been isolated are able to communicate instantaneously—which, for Kissinger, is both a good and a bad thing. On the one hand, these global interactions have allowed for the spread of new ideas that could eventually form the basis of the universal order that Kissinger so desires. On the other hand, some of these ideas—the Chinese and the Islamic above all—are inherently hostile to the prevailing Western vision of world order.

Though Kissinger identifies these different approaches to world order, he does not suggest a potential solution to the current impasse.

> *"Our age is insistently, at times almost desperately, in pursuit of a concept of world order. Chaos threatens side by side with unprecedented interdependence: the spread of weapons of mass destruction, the disintegration of states, the impact of environmental depredations [ravages], the persistence of genocidal practices, and the spread of new technologies threatening to drive conflict beyond human control or comprehension."*
>
> —— Henry Kissinger, *World Order: Reflections on the Character of Nations and the Course of History*

Approach

In order to achieve his objective, Kissinger adopts an approach that applies historical analysis in a regional manner. He starts with an examination of European history, specifically of how the Peace of Westphalia* (a series of peace treaties) that ended the Thirty Years' War* between the political body known as the Holy Roman Empire* and several other neighboring European states in 1648 contributed to the formulation of modern concepts such as sovereignty, balance of power,* and legitimacy. These are ideas that European colonial* powers—Britain, France, Portugal, Spain, and so on—subsequently adopted in their colonial empires (that is, in the territories that they claimed, governed, and exploited overseas). For this reason, the prevailing conception of world order throughout the globe is based on these Westphalian concepts, and enshrined in international institutions, most notably the United Nations.*

Simply because a Western view of world order prevails throughout the world, however, it does not mean that it is accepted universally. For this reason, Kissinger then examines Islamic, Asian (that is, Japanese and Indian), Chinese, and American conceptions of world order, which differ in many ways from that developed in Europe. In each of these instances, Kissinger uses historical analysis to show how these conceptions developed, often based on each region's historical experiences and interactions with threatening European powers. Even the American view of world order, which is technically a descendent of the Westphalian order, differs from its European cousins in that it is premised on freedom, justice, and democracy. These are concepts that Adolf Hitler* or Joseph Stalin*—both European leaders, both on the opposite extremes of the political spectrum—could hardly have accepted as legitimate even though each otherwise accepted, albeit to varying degrees, the core concepts of the Westphalian order.

Contribution in Context

It is important to bear in mind that *World Order* was written toward the end of Kissinger's illustrious career as an academic and statesman. As an academic, Kissinger's publications have consistently focused on issues that relate in one way or another to world order. For example, the first two chapters of *World Order* deal with the establishment of the Westphalian order and the conference known as the Congress of Vienna,* held in 1815 to decide a new European political order following the defeat of Napoleon Bonaparte,* the French emperor who had brought most of continental Europe under French domination. Discussions of both these topics appear in most of Kissinger's publications. Indeed both formed the basis of Kissinger's initial academic inquiry *A World Restored: Metternich, Castlereagh and the Problems of Peace, 1812–22* (1957), which analyzed the role diplomats at the Congress of Vienna played in establishing the Westphalian system as the basis of all international relations in the West. Kissinger again returned to these themes in his lengthy work on the history of diplomatic relations, *Diplomacy* (1994), which also provides an extended discussion of American foreign policy. In 2011, Kissinger published *On China*, which focuses on the history of Sino-American relations and puts forward recommendations on how the United States should approach the rise of the Chinese superpower.*

In other words, Kissinger had previously written on more than half of the topics under discussion in *World Order*.

The originality of *World Order* comes not from the material that he draws on to construct his narrative, but from how he uses this information to show that conceptions of world order are not unique to the West.

---

1. Henry Kissinger, *World Order* (New York: Penguin, 2015), 2.

SECTION 2
IDEAS

MODULE 5
MAIN IDEAS

KEY POINTS

- The main themes of *World Order* are world order,* power, and legitimacy,* themes used by Kissinger to examine the European, Islamic, Asian, and American conceptions of world order.
- Henry Kissinger argues that order needs to be cultivated through diplomacy, not imposed through military force.
- The tone of the book is deliberately accessible, intended to appeal to general readers as well as specialists. The book is far from drily academic.

Key Themes

The main themes of Henry Kissinger's *World Order* are evident in the book's title: world order itself, power, and legitimacy. *World Order* examines how historical experiences around the world have resulted in distinctly different conceptualizations—European, Islamic, Asian, and American— of these ideas.

The most dominant view of world order is that of the European concept, which stems from the Westphalian* order that was developed in the seventeenth century, following the end of Europe's Thirty Years' War (1618–48).* The Peace of Westphalia* of 1648, signed to bring the conflict to an end, introduced the concepts of balance of power* and sovereignty.*

The Islamic conception of world order* is universal, deriving its power and legitimacy from religion. This view holds that Islam is destined to expand over the realms of non-believers until the whole world is brought under a unitary system based on the teachings of the Prophet Muhammad.*[1]

The Asian order centers on multiplicity,* with several competing visions of order developing in China, Japan, and India. China viewed itself as the center of a hierarchical and universal concept of order. As Kissinger observed, "Sovereignty in the European sense did not exist, because the emperor held sway over 'All Under Heaven.'"[2] However, Japan developed separately from China even if inevitably it was influenced by its much larger neighbor. In Japan legitimacy is vested in the emperor, who is considered divine—the "Son of Heaven." However, since World War II,* Japan has adopted a largely Westphalian conception of power and legitimacy. Similarly, India, with its cultural roots based in the religion of Hinduism* rather than Chinese Confucianism* called for a multipolar* world order—a world order led by several more or less equally powerful nations—based on mutual respect, nonaggression, noninterference, equality and mutual benefit, and peaceful coexistence.[3]

Finally, the American sense of world order is derived from the European, but modified to take into consideration the concepts of freedom, justice, and American exceptionalism* (the idea that the United States stands apart from other nations, largely due to an ideology based on freedom, justice, and representative democracy): "In the American view of world order, peace and balance would occur naturally, and ancient enmities would be set aside—once other nations were given the same principled say in their own governance."[4]

> "World order describes the concept held by a region or civilization about the nature of just arrangements and the distribution of power thought to be applicable to the entire world. An international order is the practical application of these concepts to a substantial part of the globe—large enough to affect the global balance of power. Regional orders involve the same principles applied to a defined geographic area."
>
> ——Henry Kissinger, *World Order: Reflections on the Character of Nations and the Course of History*

Exploring the Ideas

The European concept of world order developed in the seventeenth century, following an extended period of war throughout the continent. As Kissinger explains, the Westphalian system was reliant on "a system of independent states refraining from interference in each other's domestic affairs and checking each other's ambitions through a general equilibrium of power."[5] Each state is assigned sovereignty—or authority and capacity to rule—over a set geographical area and acknowledges the "domestic structures and religious vocations of its fellow states as realities and refrains from challenging their existence."[6] Finally, should one state grow stronger than the other states, these other states would group together in an alliance, their combined strength allowing them to restore the balance of power.

The Islamic order finds its roots in the massive expansion of Islam from its Arabian heartlands in the seventh century following the death in 632 C.E. of Muhammad. Within 100 years, Islamic armies had conquered vast swathes of territory, from the Strait of Gibraltar (the stretch of water between North Africa and southern Spain) in the west, to parts of the Indian subcontinent in the east. As Kissinger observed, "Islam was at once a religion, a multiethnic superstate, and a new world order."[7] To those who lived within these Islamic territories—called *dar al-Islam** or "house of Islam"—it was their duty to incorporate into the Islamic empire the non-Muslim people that lived in the lands beyond—*dar al-harb** or the "realm of war." The strategy to achieve this universal view of world order is known as *jihad** ("struggle"—although often misinterpreted to mean "holy war").

    The Asian concept of world order is the oldest. Ever since its unification in 221 B.C.E., China has stood at the center of the Asian order. China viewed itself as "the sole sovereign government of the world"—that is, "all under heaven"—and its emperor as the "linchpin between the human and the divine" worlds.[8] "In this view," Kissinger notes, "world order reflected a universal hierarchy, not an equilibrium of competing sovereign states,"[9] and all other states were required to pay tribute. In other words, the Chinese emperor was the sole representative of God on earth, and all worldly states were under his dominion.

    Finally, the American conception of world order eschews traditional Westphalian concepts of balance of power and hierarchy in favor of a universal concept of order based on the principles of democracy, justice, and freedom. Referencing "manifest destiny,"* the widely held nineteenth-century doctrine that the United States was destined to expand westward from the Atlantic to the Pacific oceans, Kissinger notes: "America has played a paradoxical role in world order: it expanded across a continent in the name of manifest destiny while abjuring any imperial designs; exerted a decisive influence on momentous events while disclaiming any motivation of national interest; and became a superpower* while disavowing any intention to conduct power politics." As a result, America's concept of world order is somewhat idealistic and based on the spread of values that "it believed all other peoples aspired to replicate."[10]

Language and Expression

World Order is a commercial work, intended for a wide audience, so it is written in an accessible style designed to appeal to general readers as much as to specialists and other experts. This does not mean that either the language or the ideas explored in the book are unsophisticated. However, in comparison to earlier works such as *Diplomacy*, published in 1994, which was specifically aimed at specialists, *World Order*, much like Kissinger's 2011 book *On China*, is deliberately targeted at a much wider readership.

Kissinger, who is in his nineties, acknowledges in the text that he has staff who conduct his research and type out his manuscripts, and he is open about the level of editorial scrutiny that the text was given by his mainstream commercial publisher, Penguin, who would necessarily want the book to reach the largest possible audience. He points out that numerous colleagues, scholars, fact-checkers, acquaintances, and friends had read through the manuscript and offered editorial advice.[11] Taken together, these factors help explain why *World Order* is written in a much clearer and more comprehensible style than many of his other works.

---

1. Henry Kissinger, *World Order* (New York: Penguin, 2015), 5.
2. Kissinger, *World Order*, 4–5.
3. Kissinger, *World Order,* 205.
4. Kissinger, *World Order*, 6.
5. Kissinger, *World Order*, 3.
6. Kissinger, *World Order,* 3.
7. Kissinger, *World Order*, 99.
8. Kissinger, *World Order*, 213.
9. Kissinger, *World Order*, 213.
10. Kissinger, *World Order*, 234.
11. Kissinger, *World Order*, 375–7.

MODULE 6
SECONDARY IDEAS

KEY POINTS

- The key secondary ideas of *World Order* are balance of power* (or equilibrium), sovereignty* (the right to exercise authority), and national interests* (those things a state believes are vital to its political, military, economic, or diplomatic reputation or survival).
- Because Europe imposed the dominant international system on the world through colonialism* (the policy of seizing territories and governing them for the sake of economic and political gains), these Westphalian* concepts are central to understanding how international relations operate.
- Kissinger argues that the impact of technology is changing the emergence of a new world order.

Other Ideas

The secondary themes of Henry Kissinger's *World Order* are sovereignty, balance of power, and national interests—concepts key to Kissinger's main theme of a universal world order, which he believes has never truly existed. He also identifies key challenges that world leaders face when seeking to bring about a new world order.

The concept of sovereignty refers to the authority that a ruler, state, or nation holds to govern its citizens or those of another state, or to control a geographic territory. A key factor in determining sovereignty is recognition by other states of the authority of a ruler or government over a given territory.

An important concept in the conduct of foreign affairs is the balance of power or "power equilibrium." For example, from the perspective of the realist* school of international relations, if all nations in the world had exactly the same military capability, wars would be unlikely because no one state could defeat any other; there would be a balance of power. However, as the theory goes, should one state gain an advantage over the rest, the rest would band together to challenge the more powerful state and restore the balance.

Another key concept of *World Order* is that of national interests: the goals that a country seeks to achieve and that it believes are vital to its continued survival. For example, the economy of the United States is reliant on imported foreign oil. If a hostile entity, whether a nation or a terrorist group, controlled these sources of oil, it would have the potential to cripple the US economy. So it is in America's national interests both to prevent such a hostile entity from ever controlling its supply of oil and to build up its own oil industry to reduce its reliance on foreign sources of oil.

Kissinger points out that the traditional notion of a Westphalian state has been attacked, eroded, or dismantled in recent years. A second challenge is that the political and economic organizations of the world are at variance with each other: the economic system has become global but states have not. A final challenge is the absence of an effective mechanism for world powers to consult and cooperate on important issues.[1]

> "Westphalian principles are ... the sole generally recognized basis of what exists as a world order."
> —Henry Kissinger, *World Order: Reflections on the Character of Nations and the Course of History*

Exploring the Ideas

The Peace of Westphalia* is considered a major turning point in world history. Signed in 1648, a series of three separate treaties brought about an end to the exceptionally destructive Thirty Years' War* (1618–48). As Kissinger observed, the concept of sovereignty that emerged out of the peace involved the "right of each [nation] to choose its own domestic structure and religious orientation free from intervention."[2] Moreover, "If a state [accepts] these basic requirements, it could be recognized as an international citizen able to maintain its own culture, politics, religion, and internal policies, shielded by the international system from outside intervention."[3] This citizenship—and the recognition of citizenship—in the international community is the scaffolding of an international system built on the belief that a ruler or state has sovereignty over the territory they govern.

The peace imposed by the treaties of Westphalia in 1648 established a balance of power in Europe. As Kissinger explains: "Any international order ... must sooner or later reach an equilibrium, or else it will be in a constant state of warfare." Therefore, to avoid this outcome European statesmen recognized that a balance of the military and economic power of states was a desirable outcome of foreign policy. Kissinger identifies two ways in which a balance of power can be challenged: firstly, if a secondary state tries to "enter the ranks of the major powers and sets off a series of compensating adjustments by the other powers until a new equilibrium is established"; secondly, if a major country builds up its strength to a point where it threatens the balance of power.⁴ A good example of the first was the destabilization of the European balance of power following the unification of Germany* in 1871 and its subsequent alliance with Austria–Hungary in 1879. By 1907 this threat had prompted Britain, France, and Russia to form an alliance known as the Triple Éntente* to resist the combined forces of Germany and Austria–Hungary. The collective response of the Allies (chiefly Britain, the Soviet Union, and the United States) which led to the defeat of Nazi Germany* in World War II* is a good example of the second.

Finally, Kissinger believes that every government's job is to protect its national interests. He recognizes that the interests of one state are not always compatible with those of its allies or its enemies. He quotes the nineteenth-century British prime minister Lord Palmerston:* "We have no eternal allies, and we have no perpetual enemies. Our interests are eternal and perpetual, and those interests it is our duty to follow."⁵ In other words, a government needs to do what is best to achieve its objectives whether through diplomacy, covert action, or war.

Overlooked

Because *World Order* was published in 2014, there has not been much of an opportunity for scholars to examine the ideas and themes Kissinger puts forward in great detail. This, of course, will change in time, particularly as world events continue to change the way we understand the concept of world order.

Perhaps the one area that might be overlooked by scholars in the years to come is Kissinger's chapter dealing with the relationship between technology and world order. This chapter appeared almost as an afterthought, having been developed out of a conversation Kissinger had with a colleague. And yet it is probably the most original of all the chapters in the text, because it shows how humanity has entered a new technologically driven age. As Kissinger explained, "[every] age has ... a set of beliefs that explains the universe. Science and technology are the governing concepts of our age."[6] Indeed, since World War II and the development of computers, science and technology have brought about the start of a new age that is driven primarily by technology: the cyber age (that is, the computer-driven information age). Kissinger argues that this new age has the potential to bring about revolutionary changes to concepts of world order, both positive and negative. While most readers of the text will focus on Kissinger's examination of the different perspectives on world order, this is the one area that might be overlooked.

---

1. Henry Kissinger, *World Order* (New York: Penguin, 2015), 369–70.
2. Kissinger, *World Order*, 26.
3. Kissinger, *World Order*, 27.
4. Kissinger, *World Order*, 33.
5. Kissinger, *World Order*, 27–30.
6. Kissinger, *World Order*, 330.

MODULE 7
ACHIEVEMENT

KEY POINTS

- Henry Kissinger was successful in showing how European, Islamic, Asian, and American conceptions of world order differ due to different historical experiences.
- The most important factor enabling the success of *World Order* is Kissinger's reputation and wide knowledge of world history.
- The only factor that arguably limits the success of the text is the seemingly partisan position that Kissinger adopts on controversial issues such as Iran's nuclear program.*

Assessing the Argument

There is little question that Henry Kissinger's *World Order: Reflections on the Character of Nations and the Course of History* was successful in achieving its objective. Organizing his chapters more or less along regional lines, Kissinger weaves centuries of history together in an easily digestible manner, showing how each region developed its own particular understanding of world order, sovereignty,* legitimacy,* and how to achieve a balance of power.* The text starts off with a discussion of these core concepts before offering an overview of world history, starting first with Europe and the development of the Westphalian* system.

The text next turns to an account of the origins of the Islamic order and a discussion of Iran's unusual place in the Middle East, as both an ancient nation (Persia) with a long history of interaction with Europe and as the largest Shi'a* Muslim state (the Shi'a are followers of one of the two major branches of Islam, the Sunni* being the other). From there, Kissinger analyzes the politically multipolar* nature of Asia, looking closely at the Japanese and Indian views of world order. He then turns to a detailed discussion of the Chinese conception of world order.

In the seventh and eighth chapters Kissinger combines historical analysis with a traditional narrative of American history, focusing on American presidents such as Theodore Roosevelt* and Woodrow Wilson* and their role in shaping the American conception of world order. He highlights, too, how the United States emerged as the sole superpower* after the end of the Cold War.* Finally, Kissinger offers a chapter on the role technology will play in the shaping of a future world order, focusing on how it has both transformed the way nations interact and created new dangers.

In reading *World Order* it is quite clear that Kissinger achieves his overall objective of showing that a truly global world order has never existed and that there are considerable challenges that will need to be overcome if there is ever to be a universal conception of world order.

> *"If you think America is doing just fine, then skip ahead to the poetry reviews. If, however, you worry about a globe spinning out of control, then* World Order *is for you. It brings together history, geography, modern politics and no small amount of passion ... [This] is a* cri de coeur *from a famous skeptic, a warning to future generations from an old man steeped in the past."*
>
> ——John Micklethwait, "As the World Turns: Henry Kissinger's 'World Order,'" *New York Times*

Achievement in Context

World Order (2014) was published at a time of turmoil in international politics. Throughout 2014, geopolitical challenges to global order emerged around the world. In the Middle East, the Syrian civil war* had descended into chaos, as a three-way conflict emerged between the Syrian government, US- and Saudi-backed militants, and a radical Islamist group calling itself the Islamic State of Iraq and Syria* (ISIS), or simply the Islamic State. Quite unexpectedly, in June 2014 the Islamic State managed to seize and occupy large swathes of Syria and Iraq, including Iraq's second largest city, Mosul. In Asia, China began to flex its military and economic muscle, particularly over islands in the South China Sea. At the same time, the world's attention was fixed on the mysterious disappearance of Malaysia Airlines Flight 370;* to date, its disappearance has not been fully explained. In Eastern Europe tensions erupted following protests in Ukraine,* which toppled the Russian-backed government. During the chaos, Russia annexed the Crimean Peninsula (a territory on the northern coast of the Black Sea also known as Crimea) and civil war broke out. Further disruption was caused by the outbreak of the Ebola virus* in West Africa in March 2014, which resulted in the deaths of nearly 25,000 people.[1]

When *World Order* was published in September that year, the German diplomat Wolfgang Ischinger* noted in a review of the book that "to call *World Order* timely would be an understatement, for if there was one thing the world yearned for in 2014, it was order."² Another reviewer described the text as an "urgently written book" that serves as "a memorandum to future generations of policymakers that the next half-century will be no easier to manage than the most recent one."³

Limitations

It is a bit too early to tell whether or not *World Order* will have a major impact on the ongoing debate—both inside and outside academia—about how, if at all, a world order can be achieved. But it should be noted that, because the text consists of a broad exposition of world history, *World Order* does not face limitations of either its place or time; it could be argued that it will continue to be valuable in this regard for the foreseeable future, even if its references to events such as the emergence of ISIS and the Russian intervention in Ukraine are contemporary to 2014.

That the text is also distinctly pro-American, however, is scarcely a surprise given that Kissinger has spent his entire adult life as a champion and practitioner of American foreign policy. This is particularly the case in his chapter dealing with American–Iranian relations, where he suggests that Iran made rapid progress toward acquiring nuclear weapons during its negotiations with the five permanent members of the United Nations Security Council* (China, France, Russia, the UK, and the US) and Germany.⁴ The claim is, however, conjecture, and unsubstantiated by facts: there is no evidence that Iran is seeking to build a nuclear bomb, nor that it has made progress toward acquiring nuclear weapons. There is also considerable evidence that shows that its nuclear capacity was significantly reduced during the negotiations.⁵ And yet, Kissinger's historical account of the rise of Islam is both thoughtful and accurate, as are his chapters on Asia. Kissinger's pro-American bias, in other words, does not entirely diminish the work's usefulness.

---

1. Wolfgang Ischinger, "The World According to Kissinger: How to Defend Global Order," *Foreign Affairs* (March/April 2014), accessed October 1, 2015, https://www.foreignaffairs.com/reviews/2015-03-01/world-according-kissinger.
2. Ischinger, "The World According to Kissinger."
3. Rana Mitter, "'World Order' by Henry Kissinger–review," *Guardian*, October 1, 2014, accessed October 15, 2015, http://www.theguardian.com/books/2014/oct/01/world-order-by-henry-kissinger-review-account.
4. Henry Kissinger, *World Order* (New York: Penguin, 2015), 159.
5. Arms Control Association, "Iran Nuclear Negotiations: Separating Myth from Reality," *Issue Briefs* 7, no. 2 (January 2015), accessed November 4, 2015, https://www.armscontrol.org/issue-briefs/2015-01-23/Iran-Nuclear-Negotiations-Separating-Myth-from-Reality.

MODULE 8
PLACE IN THE AUTHOR'S WORK

KEY POINTS

- Henry Kissinger's whole life has been spent studying and engaging in global politics. This theme is present throughout his entire body of work.
- *World Order* is the work of an elderly academic, diplomat, and statesman and therefore is the product of a depth of knowledge and years of experience practicing statecraft.
- *World Order* may be Kissinger's final publication.

Positioning

Henry Kissinger's *World Order: Reflections on the Character of Nations and the Course of History* comes at the end of a long and highly successful career as both an academic and a statesman. Between 1957 and 2015, he published 14 academic works and 3 memoirs, recounting his experiences in government as the national security advisor* and secretary of state* to presidents Richard Nixon* and Gerald Ford.* As a result, *World Order* is the work of a mature thinker who has spent much of his life pondering questions of power, the equilibrium in power between the nations of the international scene, and world order.

Kissinger has always been a staunch proponent of realpolitik,* the view that policy decisions should be driven by pragmatic, rather than by moral or ideological, considerations. This is evident not just in his writings, but also in the actions he took during his time in the White House. For example, in 1972, Kissinger and Nixon, both hardliners when it came to "fighting" the Cold War,* devised a strategy to increase American power at the expense of the Soviet Union.* Recognizing that Moscow's relations with Beijing had deteriorated, they renewed diplomatic relations with China, which, in turn, forced the Soviet Union to agree to a series of bilateral (two-way) agreements, during a period often referred to as détente* (a policy implemented by the United States between 1969 and 1979 to ease tension with the Soviet Union). This move was a singularly notable diplomatic coup, allowing the US to improve relations with both the Soviet Union and China while simultaneously extricating itself from the bloody Vietnam War.*

> "Americans like the cowboy ... who rides all alone into the town, the village, with his horse and nothing else ... This amazing, romantic character suits me precisely because to be alone has always been part of my style or, if you like, my technique."
> —— Henry Kissinger, *White House Years*

Integration

Within the context of Kissinger's broader body of work, *World Order* may very well be his last publication; at the age of 92, it is impressive that he is still publishing. It is plainly evident that a common thread weaves through his work: the study of power and order in international affairs.

His first book, *A World Restored* (1957), for example, an adaptation of his doctoral thesis, focuses on the establishment of a new balance of power in Europe at the Congress of Vienna* following the defeat of the French emperor Napoleon Bonaparte* in 1815. However, it was his next book, *Nuclear Weapons and Foreign Policy* (1957), that caught the attention of policy-makers and the public. In it, Kissinger fused political and military thinking with the doctrine of limited war* to establish himself as a leading foreign-policy critic, thereby propelling him toward a career as a diplomat and statesman.[1] Once again, the focus of Kissinger's work was how to create order at a time of great political, economic, and military uncertainty.

During the 1960s, Kissinger wrote several more books that cemented his position as a public academic figure, among them *The Necessity for Choice* (1961), which argued for a flexible response to Soviet aggression using conventional forces, *The Troubled Partnership* (1965), which reappraised the nature of America's relationship with its European allies, and, just prior to entering the White House, *American Foreign Policy: Three Essays* (1969), which lays out his views on the stresses affecting American foreign-policy making.

On leaving office, Kissinger published several memoirs about his time in office: *The White House Years* (1979), *Years of Upheaval* (1982), and, much later, *Years of Renewal* (1999). In the 1980s and 1990s, Kissinger mostly published collections of essays, statements, and declassified transcripts of his time in office. In 1994 he published a massive work, *Diplomacy*, which offered a grand account of diplomatic history over the centuries—perhaps his most significant contribution to the study of diplomacy to date.

In recent years, Kissinger has readdressed himself to academic concerns, with his *On China* (2011), analyzing Chinese history in terms of foreign policy, and *World Order* (2014). Both texts focus heavily on diplomatic history and the concept of world order.

Significance

Overall, Kissinger's contributions to the study of diplomatic history and foreign policy are significant. He has stood out as a strong proponent for an interest-based form of foreign policy driven by a realistic analysis of the facts of the situation, which need to be understood within their historical context.

World Order stands out as a perfect example of his outlook. In it, Kissinger offers his readers valuable insight into the development of the four great views of world order and explains how these groups differ. This, of course, requires a great deal of research along with knowledge and empathy. It is often difficult for those who are unfamiliar with the rest of the world or their histories to understand their point of view. In *World Order*, Kissinger conveys these views in a way that's easy to understand; for those who follow the events unfolding in the Middle East, for example, his chapter "Islamism and the Middle East" offers a sound description of how Islam emerged as a powerful force in the seventh century, while going into considerable depth about the origins of modern Islamic ideology. It is certainly not the antagonistic account that may have been expected.

---

1. Hans Morgenthau, "Review: *Nuclear Weapons and Foreign Policy* by Henry A. Kissinger," *American Political Science Review* 52, no. 3 (September 1958): 842.

SECTION 3
IMPACT

MODULE 9
THE FIRST RESPONSES

KEY POINTS

* *World Order* has been praised for its contribution to the debate over world order,* but criticized for Kissinger's failure to offer critical appraisals of living presidents such as George W. Bush* or Barack Obama.*
* Because the text was published in 2014, there has not yet been enough time for a debate to emerge in response to the text.
* The most important factor shaping the reception of *World Order* is Kissinger's controversial reputation, with those who dislike him writing negative reviews and those who agree with him writing positive ones.

Criticism

Because *World Order: Reflections on the Character of Nations and the Course of History* was written by a notably controversial figure in Henry Kissinger, it was bound to be reviewed by many of the major media outlets and by members of America's foreign-policy elite. Due to Kissinger's notoriety as a hard-nosed realist,* who has been accused of human-rights abuses in several countries due to decisions he made while in office,[1] there are plenty of people who dislike him on personal or ideological grounds. The majority of reviews, however, were quite positive. The former secretary of state Hillary Clinton,* for example, a politician who subscribes to a different political philosophy in the field of international relations, wrote that *World Order* "is vintage Kissinger, with his singular combination of breadth and acuity along with his knack for connecting headlines to trend lines."2

Nevertheless, the most commonly cited critique of *World Order* stems from Kissinger's steadfast refusal to be critical of living presidents, particularly George W. Bush. In particular, reviews—such as the one in the *Economist*—took exception to his "sugaring his criticism of living statesmen with compliments that are, presumably, designed to spare the client's embarrassment."3 For example, instead of offering justifiable criticism of the Bush administration's handling of the Iraq War,* Kissinger wrote: "I want to express here my continuing respect and personal affection for [Bush], who guided America with courage, dignity, and conviction in an unsteady time."4 Referring to the former US president Woodrow Wilson,* known for his role in reconstructing Europe after World War I,* the journalist James Traub* shared the *Economist*'s concern, pointing out his disbelief that Kissinger would lavish "praise on the most reckless of Wilsonian [idealists]* of them all, George W. Bush."5

> "[World Order] *is a book that every member of Congress should be locked in a room with—and forced to read before taking the oath of office."*
> —— John Micklethwait, "As the World Turns: Henry Kissinger's 'World Order'," *New York Times*

Responses

There are several reasons why it seems unlikely that Kissinger will respond to critiques of *World Order*. First, the book was published in September 2014 and so there has not been a lot of time for a critical academic engagement of the topic, largely because it can take over a year for academic book reviews to make their way through the peer review editing process.

Secondly, as a major public figure, Kissinger is not someone who tends to respond to criticism, especially from individuals such as the international relations scholar Anne-Marie Slaughter* with whom he disagrees on ideological grounds. That is not his style; rather, Kissinger is the type of scholar who publishes a book and then travels around the world giving public talks at highly regarded universities and institutions, often carefully orchestrated so that questions are searching but not overtly hostile.

A final reason why Kissinger is unlikely to respond to criticism of his text is that at his advanced age, he is unlikely to change his views even when confronted with the most persuasive alternative. As a result, it seems highly unlikely that a critical dialogue between Kissinger and his critics will ever take place over this text.

Conflict and Consensus

A more plausible intellectual outcome of the text's publication is an advance of the debate between realists and idealists, who have different conceptions of world order. Realists like Kissinger believe that foreign policy needs to reflect an assertion of power, which in turn needs to rest on legitimacy.* For example, even though Kissinger supported the US-led invasion of Iraq in 2003 that led to the Iraq War,* believing that the United States needed to project its power following the terrorist attacks of September 11, 2001 (9/11),* he also recognized that the absence of weapons of mass destruction* destroyed the legitimacy of this policing action. In short, power is not enough in itself; it must also be legitimate. To those who subscribe to Kissinger's world view, of whom there are many, the projection of power trumps any idealistic notions of cooperation.

It is at this juncture that the real debate between realists and idealists exists. For example, Anne-Marie Slaughter's outright rejection of Kissinger's work is a reflection of her belief that legitimacy takes precedence over the projection of power. In her view, foreign policy needs to be based on moral considerations and never at the expense of legitimacy. She believes that states have a responsibility to protect citizens not just at home but around the world and, if needed, states should take action to prevent atrocities, like those being committed in Syria.*6

The differences between these two camps will not be reconciled easily and will continue to shape debates about American foreign policy into the future.

---

1. Daniel Marans, "Henry Kissinger Just Turned 92. Here's Why He's Careful About Where He Travels," *Huffington Post*, May 27, 2015, accessed October 9, 2015, http://www.huffingtonpost.com/2015/05/27/henry-kissinger-human-rights_n_7454172.html.
2. Hillary Clinton, "Hillary Clinton Reviews Henry Kissinger's *World Order*," *Washington Post*, September 4, 2014, accessed September 18, 2015, https://www.washingtonpost.com/opinions/hillary-

clinton-reviews-henry-kissingers-world-order/2014/09/04/b280c654-31ea-11e4-8f02-03c644b2d7d0_story.html.

3. *Economist*, "A Bit of a Mess," September 6, 2014, accessed September 10, 2015, http://www.economist.com/news/books-and-arts/21615478-geopolitics-henry-kissinger-grand-and-gloomy-bit-mess.

4. Henry Kissinger, *World Order* (New York: Penguin, 2015), 325.

5. James Traub, "Book Review: *World Order* by Henry Kissinger," *Wall Street Journal*, September 5, 2014, accessed September 18, 2015, http://www.wsj.com/articles/book-review-world-order-by-henry-kissinger-1409952751.

6. Anne-Marie Slaughter, "How to Fix America's Foreign Policy," *New Republic*, November 19, 2014, accessed September 18, 2015, http://www.newrepublic.com/article/120030/world-order-review-what-obama-should-learn-kissingers-book.

MODULE 10
THE EVOLVING DEBATE

KEY POINTS
- It is too early to tell what *World Order* will add to the debate about how to bring about a new world order;* the book is more a history of a concept rather than the assertion of a profound argument.
- *World Order* engages directly with two main schools of thought—realism* and liberal internationalism*—while drawing on arguments from both.
- Besides its positive initial reception, *World Order* has not yet had a major impact on the debate about world order.

Uses and Problems

As one of the leading voices on American foreign policy since the early 1950s, Henry Kissinger expresses ideas in *World Order: Reflections on the Character of Nations and the Course of History* that are the product of a lifetime of scholarship, careful consideration, and debate. This analysis of an important topic—world order—from a highly respected and influential statesman, was a timely addition to an ongoing debate about how to bring about a sense of order in a world plagued with disorder.

Since the text was only published in September 2014, it is still too early to determine how Kissinger will further develop the ideas he puts forward in it. The debate over how best to forge a viable new world order has not lessened with the text's publication, with liberal internationalists arguing in favor of a strengthening of international institutions, while realists seek ways to project power, often through the use of force. More problematically, some elements in the US, such as the neoconservatives* (those who subscribe to a political philosophy characterized by an emphasis on free-market capitalism* and an interventionist foreign policy) actively oppose liberal internationalism and have sought to undermine the very institutions that liberal internationalists are trying to build up.

While Kissinger's position on how to bring about a new world order tends to fall somewhat closer to the liberal understanding, he remains an advocate of projecting American power. It will be interesting to see if Kissinger is able to explore this position further in subsequent publications over the coming years.

> *"A values-based foreign policy can be perfectly pragmatic and prudent. It makes no sense, ever, to engage in an activity in which the costs clearly outweigh the benefits."*
> ——Anne-Marie Slaughter, "How to Fix America's Foreign Policy," *New Republic*

Schools of Thought

Kissinger has long been a key figure in the debate among scholars of international relations, particularly among those who deal with American foreign policy, which pits realists against idealists. These two schools of thought are very broad, incorporating several subsets, and inherently antagonistic. Of the two, Kissinger is an outspoken champion of realism, but a closer examination of the ideas put forward in *World Order* suggests that he might actually represent a bridge between the two. As the former US secretary of state* Hillary Clinton* noted in her positive review of *World Order*, Kissinger believed that for an international order to take hold and last, "it must relate 'power to legitimacy.'"* To her, this admission "sounds surprisingly idealistic."[1] She is right. Though Kissinger identifies himself as a realist, he proposes that America is at its strongest when it stands up for what he believes to be American values—freedom, justice, and democracy—and its conception of world order.

To Kissinger, an important objective of US policy should be to bring about a "world order of states affirming individual dignity and participatory governance, and cooperating internationally in accordance with agreed-upon rules."[2] Even if this is a remarkably idealist objective, Kissinger is not naïve; he recognizes that the journey to a new world order will be fraught with challenges, some of which may require military force. While idealists no longer challenge this notion, the real point of contention today is under what circumstances force should be used. For modern idealists such as Anne-Marie Slaughter,* force should be used in instances where governments have failed to protect their own citizens, following the so-called Responsibility to Protect* (R2P) doctrine (the doctrine in international relations according to which a state that fails to protect its citizens from human rights violations forfeits its sovereignty,* meaning that the international community has the right to intervene). Kissinger, on the other hand, believes force should be used in instances where a nation's national interests* are threatened and efforts at diplomacy have failed to bring about a negotiated settlement.

In Current Scholarship

Although Kissinger has many admirers among America's foreign policy elite, even among those who do not typically agree with him, such as Bill Clinton,* it would be inaccurate to say that a school of thought or a group of disciples has developed around *World Order* so soon after its publication. This does not, however, mean that *World Order* does not fit in with the work of other realists, such as the international relations scholars Fareed Zakaria* or John Mearsheimer,* who both tend to approach American foreign policy questions about power, legitimacy, and national interests through the lens of history.

In June 2013, for example, Zakaria posted a video that places the Syrian civil war* in a historical context, pointing out that it is the last of three minority-dominated states in the Middle East that have undergone traumatic transitions to majority rule, following the Lebanese Civil War* (1975–90) and Iraq* after the US-led invasion in 2003, and warns that it will take at least a decade to resolve the Syrian tragedy. He uses history to argue against an American intervention in Syria, because deposing the regime would then lead to a power struggle among countless factions, of which the Islamic State of Iraq and Syria* (ISIS) is the most powerful.[3]

Mearsheimer offered a similar explanation for the crisis following the collapse of the Ukrainian* government and the subsequent annexation of the Crimean Peninsula by Russia in 2014.

Arguing against the conventional wisdom that the crisis was a product of Russian aggression, Mearsheimer said that "the United States and its European allies share most of the responsibility for the crisis" due to their strategy of drawing the Ukraine* into the Western orbit, a move that Russian leaders had repeatedly opposed. [4]

1. Hillary Clinton, "Hillary Clinton Reviews Henry Kissinger's *World Order*," *Washington Post*, September 4, 2014, accessed September 18, 2015, https://www.washingtonpost.com/opinions/hillary-clinton-reviews-henry-kissingers-world-order/2014/09/04/b280c654-31ea-11e4-8f02-03c644b2d7d0_story.html.
2. Henry Kissinger, *World Order* (New York: Penguin, 2015), 373.
3. Fareed Zakaria, "Ask Fareed Zakaria Anything: Stay Out of Syria," *The Dish*, June 7, 2013, accessed October 16, 2015, http://dish.andrewsullivan.com/2013/06/07/ask-fareed-zakaria-anything-stay-out-of-syria/.
4. John Mearsheimer, "Why the Ukraine Crisis is the West's Fault," *Foreign Affairs* (September/October 2014), accessed October 16, 2015, http:// www.foreignaffairs.com/articles/141769/john-j-mearsheimer/why-the-ukraine-crisis-is-the-wests-fault.

MODULE 11
IMPACT AND INFLUENCE TODAY

KEY POINTS

- Today, *World Order* stands out as a great introductory text for students of world history and international politics.
- The main challenge to Kissinger's ideas comes from liberal internationalists* who argue that he has failed to recognize the importance of the Responsibility to Protect* doctrine (according to which the international community has the right to intervene if a state fails to protect its citizens from human rights violations).
- Kissinger has not responded directly to this challenge.

Position

As part of the contemporary debate about how to bring about a new world order,* Henry Kissinger's *World Order: Reflections on the Character of Nations and the Course of History* offers his readers a broad overview of the main issues at play, but fails to provide a thoughtful way forward. This fault seems to be by design. The text was never meant to advocate a specific set of recommendations about how the United States should force its own vision of world order on the rest of the world; rather, it looks to history to detail the challenges that future generations face in constructing such a new order. In that sense, Kissinger's text is an important guide on how to navigate modern global politics, not a remedy to the world's many problems.

For this reason, there is no set consensus as to the text's importance in terms of the wider debate between realists,* like

Kissinger, and liberal internationalists, who argue that the best way to establish a new order is to strengthen international institutions. While Kissinger is by no means opposed to international institutions like the United Nations,* his neoconservative* colleagues in the Republican Party* such as Paul Wolfowitz* or John Bolton,* do not share this view. They argue that the US needs to impose order on the world through force, as was intended to happen with the Iraq War.* In this sense, Kissinger's work emerges as a sort of bridge between the idealist* and multilateralist* vision of order on the left and the realist and unilateralist* view on the right. To Kissinger, international institutions need to be strengthened, but he also contends that states reserve the right to use force when state or non-state actors, such as the Islamic State of Iraq and Syria* (ISIS), threaten their national interests.

> "The irony—and enduring tragedy—of Kissinger's insistence on upholding the Westphalian norm of absolute sovereignty is that the responsibility to protect is actually an heir to the Peace of Westphalia."
>
> —— Anne-Marie Slaughter, "How to Fix America's Foreign Policy," *New Republic*

Interaction

As a work premised on realist assumptions, *World Order* stands somewhat opposed to liberal internationalist views of a world order premised on cooperation. The most outspoken challenger of the views expressed in Kissinger's *World Order* is Anne-

Marie Slaughter,* a professor of international affairs at Princeton University who served as director of policy planning in the US department of state (the government department dealing with foreign affairs). She argues that Kissinger's belief in a power-based foreign policy fails to take into consideration recent progress toward the establishment of a new conception of world order in which Westphalian* principles are renovated in the form of a relatively new foreign policy concept called the Responsibility to Protect* (R2P). Slaughter believes that states have an obligation under the Universal Declaration of Human Rights* to intervene when governments are no longer able to protect their citizens. Her gripe with Kissinger stems from his "insistence on upholding the Westphalian norm of absolute sovereignty."* And that what he does not realize "is that the responsibility to protect is actually an heir to the Peace of Westphalia (1648)."*

"In an age in which the single greatest threat of the use of force against innocent civilians usually comes not from a foreign government but from their own, the responsibility to protect is an essential corollary to the Westphalian commandments. It amends the very idea of absolute sovereignty, holding states accountable at least for mass murder."[1]

In short, Slaughter argues that Kissinger fails to realize that a new world order is already beginning to take shape, largely because it does not fit with his own conception of world order.

The Continuing Debate

There is no end in sight in the ongoing debate between liberal* and neoconservative visions of world order, as the ideological divide between the two has been exacerbated by partisan politics in the United States. The centrality of the debate over world order has recently centered on the Middle East, where the rise of the Islamic State of Iraq and Syria (ISIS) has disrupted the regional order. With no end to the crisis in sight, Kissinger put forward a set of recommendations on how the Obama* administration can get itself out of a deteriorating situation in the Middle East in a recent article. He wrote: "American policy has sought to straddle the motivations of all parties and is therefore on the verge of losing the ability to shape events. The US is now opposed to, or at odds in some way or another with, all parties in the region: with Egypt on human rights; with Saudi Arabia over Yemen; with each of the Syrian parties over different objectives. The US proclaims the determination to remove [Syrian president Bashar al-Assad*] but has been unwilling to generate effective leverage—political or military—to achieve that aim."[2]

Kissinger believes that "as long as ISIS survives and remains in control of a geographically defined territory, it will compound all Middle East tensions" and argues that "the destruction of ISIS is more urgent than the overthrow of Bashar al-Assad." This proposal is firmly rooted in Kissinger's belief in the projection of American power, which is why he laments the Obama administration's acquiescence to Russia's military intervention in Syria in the fall of 2015.[3]

Slaughter takes a slightly different position. While she agrees with Kissinger that the United States needs to do something in

Syria, she disagrees on the end objective. Whereas Kissinger believes the objective is destroying ISIS, Slaughter believes that it should be limited to saving the lives of innocent civilians, which is why she has called for the United States and its allies to establish a "no-fly zone" or "safe zone" in Syria to protect civilians and take steps to stave off a growing humanitarian crisis.[4]

Both of these perspectives underscore the nuanced differences between realists and liberal internationalists.

---

1. Anne-Marie Slaughter, "How to Fix America's Foreign Policy," *New Republic*, November 19, 2014, accessed September 18, 2015, http://www. newrepublic.com/article/120030/world-order-review-what-obama-should-learn-kissingers-book.
2. Henry Kissinger, "A Path Out of the Middle East Collapse," *Wall Street Journal*, October 16, 2015, accessed October 22, 2015, http://www.wsj. com/articles/a-path-out-of-the-middle-east-collapse-1445037513.
3. Kissinger, "A Path Out of the Middle East Collapse."
4. Anne-Marie Slaughter, "A No-Fly Zone for Syria," *Project Syndicate*, August 25, 2015, accessed October 22, 2015, http://www.project-syndicate.org/commentary/no-fly-zone-syria-by-anne-marie-slaughter-2015-08.

MODULE 12
WHERE NEXT?

KEY POINTS

- *World Order* is an important and timely contribution to an ongoing debate about the nature of world order* and how to bring about a new world order.
- Looking ahead, *World Order* will continue to be an important text because it has revitalized an important debate about world order, one that had been stagnating.
- Importantly, *World Order* internationalizes the debate about the nature of world order, explaining to readers that other conceptions of world order exist that differ from their own.

Potential

Henry Kissinger's *World Order: Reflections on the Character of Nations and the Course of History* is designed for those interested in the past but concerned about the future. The text offers its readers an immensely valuable telling of world history, while explaining the origins, nuances, and challenges of some of the world's greatest civilizations. The value of this comes from the notion that the best way to predict the future is to have a strong understanding of the past. This is precisely what Kissinger's text provides for its readers.

While it seems unlikely that Kissinger will modify or update this text, it has potential to spark a debate among other diplomatic historians and scholars of international relations about how to create a new, universal world order. This is fertile ground for young scholars, who might be interested in developing theories on how to bring this about. Unfortunately, the book's conclusion fails to offer a potential strategy about what this new world order might be—which is perhaps the spark that other scholars needed to contend with, if only by offering potential alternatives. Over time, however, it is possible that this could be an area of considerable intellectual debate.

> "Kissinger's secret wish might be to stage a Congress of Vienna for the twenty-first century. And although world politics is complicated by a host of factors that don't fit easily into the Westphalian model—transnational identities, digital hyperconnectivity, weapons of mass destruction, global terrorist networks—Kissinger is still right to insist [in World Order] that the management of great-power relations remains of paramount importance."
>
> ——Wolfgang Ischinger, "The World According to Kissinger," *Foreign Affairs*

Future Directions

At this point, it is difficult to ascertain which scholars will emerge as successors to Kissinger, particularly among those who engage in broad conceptual studies relating to concepts such as world order, sovereignty,* or balance of power.* However, it seems likely that such a successor or successors would come from the field of international relations as opposed to diplomatic history. This is because diplomatic historians, quite logically, focus on the past and rarely deal with conceptual debates about the future. While this is what separates Kissinger from most diplomatic historians, this is surely a by-product of his considerable experience as a policy-maker and his subsequent work as a political consultant for governments around the world.

In international relations, however, scholars are actively engaged in theoretical debates about the nature of relations between states, non-state actors such as international corporations and terrorist groups, and nongovernmental organizations such as the United Nations* and the World Bank.* Within this field, there are a number of theoretical variants, such as classical realism,* neorealism,* neoliberalism,* neoclassical realism,* and liberal internationalism.* Of these, neoclassical realism is the closest fit to Kissinger's outlook, realpolitik,* which focuses on maximizing power and protecting interests without concerns about morality. With this in mind, any scholar wishing to build upon Kissinger's *World Order* would probably come from this school of thought. Within the field of international relations, the most likely candidates are the political scientists John Mearsheimer,* Stephen Walt,* Robert Kagan,* Vali Nasr,* Francis Fukuyama,* and Anne-Marie Slaughter,* though in each case they would almost certainly approach the matter from different perspectives.

Summary

Kissinger's *World Order* offers an excellent insight into one of the central problems facing the world today: how to bring about a sense of order. The text presents its readers with an astute analysis of the four main views of world order: the European Westphalian* system, premised on the concepts of sovereignty, legitimacy,* and balance of power; the universalist Islamic concept of order,* which historically has pitted Muslims against non-Muslims in a competition for dominance; the Chinese system,* according to which China and its power stands as the primary source of order; and the American conception, which is rooted in the belief that freedom, justice, and democracy are universal concepts that can be applied around the world. It also offers a thought-provoking discussion of the role that technology has played as a source of inspiration (for example, in bringing people together by means of telecommunication networks) and of disruption (for example, posting videos of terrorist attacks) in the quest for world order. This discussion offers valuable insight into the challenges that world leaders face in seeking to forge a new world order.

Even though *World Order* is steeped in world history, the singular way in which Kissinger explains why each conception of world order differs from the other is valuable to anyone interested in understanding the world today—or for anyone concerned about where it is heading tomorrow.

GLOSSARY OF TERMS

1. **9/11:** on September 11, 2001, two commercial airliners hijacked by Islamic fundamentalist terrorists were flown into the World Trade Center in New York, killing approximately 3,000 people. A third hijacked airliner was crashed into the Pentagon and a fourth went down in a field in Pennsylvania.

2. **Afghanistan War (2001–):** the military intervention by North Atlantic Treaty Organization (NATO) and allied forces following the September 11 attacks on America.

3. **Al-Qaeda:** a militant Islamic fundamentalist group that was behind the terrorist attack against the United States on September 11, 2001.

4. **American exceptionalism:** a belief that the United States stands apart from other nations, largely due to an ideology based on freedom, justice, and representative democracy.

5. **Anarchy:** a state of leaderlessness; sovereign states exist in an anarchic or self-regulatory world where there is no authority compelling them one way or another.

6. **Authoritarian:** in governmental terms, a system in which governmental authority intrudes into the citizen's life at the expense of liberty.

7. **Balance of power:** in the field of international relations, the extent to which the power of one state is balanced by the equivalent power of another state or states.

8. **Berlin Wall:** a barrier that divided Berlin from 1961 to 1989 and came to symbolize the efforts of the Soviet Union to block itself and its satellite states from the West.

9. **Boko Haram:** an Islamic militant group founded in 2002 and operating in northern Nigeria. It has been fighting an insurgency since 2009, but captured global attention in April 2014 when it kidnapped 276 young girls from a school.

10. **Capitalism:** an economic system in which privately owned goods and services are exchanged for profit.

11. **Classical realism:** a school of international relations theory that assumes state action is agent-driven (controlled by leaders, rather than the structure of the system), and identifies the inherent imperfections of human nature as the source

of conflict.

12. **Cold War (1947–91):** a period of tension between the United States and its Western allies and the Eastern federation of countries known as the Soviet Union, marked by the threat of nuclear war, proxy conflicts (meaning conflicts started by two nations that do not directly engage with each other), espionage, and so on.

13. **Colonialism:** refers to a policy whereby one country takes full or partial political control over another country and occupies it with colonists. It often involved unequal power relations between the ruler (colonist) and ruled (colony), and the economic exploitation of the colonies.

14. **Communism:** a political ideology that advocates state ownership of the means of production, the collectivization of labor, and the abolition of social class. It was the ideology of the Soviet Union (1922–91) and stood in contrast to free-market capitalism during the Cold War.

15. **Confucianism:** an Asian philosophical and ethical system founded by the Chinese philosopher Confucius 2,500 years ago.

16. **Congress of Vienna (1814–15):** an international conference held in Vienna, Austria, before and after the final defeat of the French emperor and military leader Napoleon Bonaparte. The conference's purpose was to reestablish a stable political order and balance of power in Europe.

17. ***Dar al-harb*:** the "realm of war"; a historical term denoting the territories of non-Muslims bordering *dar al-Islam* that needed to be incorporated into the Islamic empire.

18. ***Dar al-Islam*:** "house of Islam"; that is, the territories of the Islamic empire that emerged in the seventh century.

19. **Détente:** a policy implemented by the United States between 1969 and 1979 to deal with the Soviet Union. The policy consisted of easing tensions through less provocative behavior and interaction through meetings and summits.

20. **Eastern Bloc:** refers to a grouping of socialist states, mostly in Eastern Europe, which were dominated by the Soviet Union until the late 1980s.

21. **Ebola virus outbreak:** an epidemic of the Ebola virus that swept through West

Africa in 2014 killing almost 25,000 people, creating a worldwide panic that it could spread.

22. **Geostrategy:** the study of the ways in which strategy and geography shape politics and international relations.

23. **GI Bill:** a piece of US legislation adopted during World War II that provided benefits to ex-servicemen, such as low-interest loans and bursaries to cover living expenses and the costs of further education tuition.

24. **Greenpeace:** founded in Canada in 1971, it is an international organization that uses civil disobedience as a tactic to bring about awareness of environmental issues to the public and world leaders.

25. **Hegemony:** a situation where a single state or individual is able to dominate all others. For example, in the aftermath of the Cold War the United States was considered the global hegemon.

26. **Hinduism:** is a major polytheistic (that is, a belief in more than one god) world religion, practiced by over a billion people worldwide; its heartland is in the Indian subcontinent.

27. **Holy Roman Empire:** a central European political body composed of a number of states, formed during the early medieval period and dissolved in the first decade of the nineteenth century.

28. **Idealism:** a theory of international relations holding that states should apply their own internal philosophy to the conduct of international relations. This theory is closely associated with the 28th US president Woodrow Wilson, in office between 1913 and 1921, who argued that all people should have the right to determine their own destiny.

29. **Iran's nuclear program:** since the early 1990s, Western powers have accused Iran of developing nuclear weapons. The Iranian government has maintained that it has a right to develop peaceful nuclear technology and has denied a nuclear weapons programme. Negotiations about the issue have taken place periodically since 2003.

30. **Iraq War (2003–11):** an armed conflict primarily between the United States

and its allies and Iraq. After toppling the government of Saddam Hussein in 2003, the conflict descended into a sectarian civil war, which pitted Iraq's Shi'a and Sunni populations against each other. In December 2011, American forces withdrew from Iraq.

31. **Islamic State of Iraq and Syria (ISIS):** a radical Islamist militant group that seized control of large swathes of territory in Iraq and Syria in 2014, and is also known to operate in eastern Libya, the Sinai Peninsula of Egypt, and other areas of the Middle East and North Africa.

32. ***Jihad*:** an Islamic term that means "struggle." Often mistranslated as holy war, it means to struggle against an obstacle, whether against nonbelievers or with any kind of challenge in life.

33. **Lebanese Civil War (1975–90):** a conflict waged in Lebanon after the collapse of central authority in 1975.

34. **Legitimacy:** to be lawful; to be accepted as lawful.

35. **Liberal:** as a political philosophy, liberalism emphasizes the importance of individual liberty and equality; its roots are in the period of European intellectual history known as the Enlightenment (late-seventeenth to late-eighteenth century), in which oppressive and hereditary forms of governmental power were challenged.

36. **Liberal internationalism:** a school of international relations theory that suggests states can achieve peace and mutual cooperation if policies promoting international structures fostering a liberal world order are pursued.

37. **Limited war:** a military concept used to describe a type of warfare, where strategic objectives and the scale of effort are limited. This concept is often contrasted with total war, where all the resources of a nation are geared toward ensuring total victory over an opponent. World War II is the best example of total war, whereas the 1990–91 Gulf War was limited to forcing Iraq to withdraw from Kuwait.

38. **Malaysia Airlines Flight 370:** on March 8, 2014 an airplane from the Malaysian capital, Kuala Lumpur, disappeared, leading to one of the largest

search missions in history. No survivors were found, and only a small piece of wreckage was located more than a year later.

39. **Manifest destiny:** a doctrine developed in the nineteenth century in the United States that was used to justify the expansion of the country westward across North America.

40. **Multilateralism:** three or more nations working together toward an objective. Contrasted with bilateral (between two nations) or unilateral (a nation alone).

41. **Multiplicity:** a concept used to describe a situation where there are multiple poles of power in a given region (Asia, for example, where Russia, China, India, and Japan are all considered centers of power).

42. **Multipolarity:** a distribution of power within the international system; a multipolar system has power concentrated among three or more states. A bipolar system has power concentrated in two states, and a unipolar system is the dominance of a single state (also known as hegemony).

43. **Mutually assured destruction:** a phrase used during the Cold War to describe the belief that an attack by one superpower on the other would lead to the destruction of both, as each possessed the ability to launch retaliatory attacks after the first strike through nuclear armed aircraft or submarines.

44. **National interests:** a concept in international relations that describes something a state believes is vital to its political, military, economic, or diplomatic reputation or survival.

45. **National security advisor:** the chief advisor to the president of the United States for matters related to national security, foreign policy, and defense.

46. **Nazi Germany (1933–45):** Germany under the rule of Adolf Hitler, an extreme nationalist politician who sought to unify all the German-speaking people under one state and revise the European and global order. Hitler's aggressive and anti-Semitic policies led to World War II, the Holocaust (the systematic slaughter of millions of European Jews) and the deaths of perhaps 50 million people.

47. **Neoclassical realism:** a combination of neorealism and classical realism. Its supporters hold that state action can be explained with reference to both structural

factors (such as the distribution of capabilities—military, economic, political, etc.—between states) and agent-driven factors (such as the ambitions of given leaders).

48. **Neoconservatism:** a political ideology characterized by an emphasis on free-market capitalism and an interventionist foreign policy. Examples of prominent neoconservatives are Paul Wolfowitz, Donald Rumsfeld, and John Bolton.

49. **Neoliberalism:** a school of international relations theory holding that cooperation among countries is possible and likely, especially through international institutions, because states prefer to maximize their absolute gains rather than their relative gains over one another.

50. **Neorealism:** a school of international relations theory assuming that structural constraints (like the distribution of world power) rather than human agency will determine actor behavior.

51. **Nobel Peace Prize:** an annual prize awarded to an individual or individuals who have devoted themselves to bringing about peaceful relations between nations. Notable winners include Henry Kissinger, Martin Luther King, Jr., Nelson Mandela, Jimmy Carter, Barack Obama, and Malala Yousafzai.

52. **Offensive realism:** a theoretical concept according to which the international system is anarchical; great powers are the main actors in global politics; all states possess offensive capabilities; another state's intentions can never be certain; survival is the primary objective; and all states are rational actors (that is, primarily concerned with their own interests).

53. **Othering:** the process of creating a collective identity ("Islamic Iran," for example) against an imaginative construction (in this case, "the Christian West"). This approach is often used in international relations, where states point out the negative attributes of their neighbors to emphasize their own strengths.

54. **Peace of Westphalia (1648):** a series of peace accords that ended the Thirty Years' War, signed simultaneously in Osnabrück and Münster in Germany. It helped to solidify the modern world order, whereby all states are considered equal and interstate aggression was to be solved by the establishment of a balance of power.

55. **Realism:** a school of international relations theory according to which states are the primary actors; states all share the goal of survival; and states provide for their own security.

56. **Realpolitik:** a German term meaning, literally, "the politics of real things" denoting a concept in international relations that policy decisions should be driven by pragmatic—not moral or ideological—considerations.

57. **Republican Party:** a right-wing political party in the United States founded in 1854; former Republican presidents include George H. W. Bush, George W. Bush, Richard Nixon, and Ronald Reagan.

58. **Responsibility to Protect (R2P):** a concept in international relations arguing that a state that fails to protect its citizens from human-rights violations forfeits its sovereignty and that the international community accordingly has the right to intervene.

59. **Secretary of state:** the head of the US department of state; a cabinet level position in the US government; and the chief American diplomat.

60. **Shi'a and Sunni Islam:** the two main branches of Islam, a religion that split into two main factions after the death of the Prophet Muhammad in c.e. 632. Sunni Islam is the largest religious denomination of any world religion. Shi'a Islam (sometimes written as Shia in English) or Shi'ism, is the second largest sect of Islam, with a minority of around 11 percent. The differences between the sects are mostly derived from their different historical experiences, political and social developments, and ethnic composition. Shi'ites reject the first three Sunni caliphs (leaders) and regard the fourth caliph, Ali, as the prophet's true successor.

61. **Sino-centric:** an ideology holding that China stands at the center of the world.

62. **Sovereignty:** the right to govern a specific territory.

63. **Soviet Union (1922–91):** the Union of Soviet Socialist Republics (USSR), often shortened to "Soviet Union," had its roots in the Russian Revolution of 1917, which overthrew the czarist regime of the Russian Empire. In 1922, a Communist regime led by Vladimir Lenin established the Soviet Union after prevailing in a military conflict against anti-revolution parties.

64. **Superpower:** a term, first coined in 1944, to describe an exceptionally powerful and influential nation, often used to refer to the United States and the Soviet Union during the Cold War, when both states were the two most powerful nations in the world.

65. **Syrian Civil War (2011–):** a civil conflict in Syria that began as part of the Arab Spring in 2010. The conflict is between the Alawite-dominated Ba'athist Syrian government of Bashar al-Assad and several Sunni factions, which are backed by a range of foreign powers such as the United States and the Gulf States. However, beginning in 2014 the Islamic State emerged as the most powerful nongovernmental faction.

66. **Thirty Years' War (1618–48):** a European conflict between the Holy Roman Empire and several Protestant Germanic states that escalated into a near Europe-wide conflict.

67. **Triple Éntente:** an alliance formed originally between Britain, the Russian Empire, and France in 1907 in response to the growth of German power in Europe. This alliance lasted through World War I.

68. **Ukraine War (2014–):** a war that began following the collapse of the Ukrainian government when Russia annexed the Crimean Peninsula and occupied parts of eastern Ukraine.

69. **Unification of Germany:** the incorporation of all the small Germanic states of central Europe into a single German state under Wilhelm I of Prussia, head of state of the most powerful nation, Prussia. It significantly altered the balance of power in Europe.

70. **Unilateralism:** a concept in international relations used to describe a situation in which a nation acts alone.

71. **United Nations:** an international organization of countries set up in 1945 to promote international peace, security, and cooperation.

72. **United Nations Security Council:** permanent body of the United Nations looking to maintain peace and security. It consists of 15 members, of which 5 (China, France, Russia, the UK, and the US) are permanent and have the power

of veto. The other members are elected for two-year terms.

73. **Universal Declaration of Human Rights:** a resolution adopted by the United Nations in 1948 that establishes a universal description of basic human rights.

74. **Universalist Islamic order:** A conception of Islam as a universalist religion, meaning that its adherents believe their view is absolute and that anyone who does not share their religion is an infidel.

75. **Vietnam War (1955–75):** a Cold War conflict between the United States and the forces of North Vietnam. In 1973 the US signed a peace treaty and withdrew its forces from South Vietnam, which collapsed two years later.

76. **War on Terror:** a term commonly applied to American-led actions throughout the Middle East against non-state "terrorist" actors, including al-Qaeda, following the attacks on the World Trade Center on September 11, 2001. The drone campaign in Pakistan, the occupation of Afghanistan, and other covert and overt operations are rolled into this effort.

77. **Weapons of mass destruction:** a term referring to weaponry capable of killing large amounts of people easily. It typically refers to biological, chemical, or nuclear weapons.

78. **Weimar Republic:** the constitutional state that was formed following the defeat of Germany in World War I and lasted until the coming to power of Adolf Hitler in 1933.

79. **Westphalian system:** the order governing European international relations since the signing of the peace accords of 1648 that ended the Thirty Years' War, signed simultaneously in Osnabrück and Münster in Germany. According to the accords, states are considered equal and interstate aggression was to be solved by the establishment of a balance of power. The system, imposed on the rest of the world during the colonial period, is premised on the concepts of sovereignty, legitimacy, and balance of power.

80. **World Bank:** an international financial institution originally set up in the aftermath of World War II to help finance the reconstruction of Europe. Today, it is used to help developing countries receive loans aimed at development projects

and reducing poverty.

81. **World order:** roughly, a stable system governing international relations based on consensus regarding the obligations and the limits of national power and so on.

82. **World War I (1914–18):** a global conflict fought between the Central Powers (Germany, Austria-Hungary, and the Ottoman Empire) and the victorious Allied Powers (Britain, France, Russia, and, after 1917, the United States). More than 16 million people would die as a result of the war.

83. **World War II (1939–45):** a global conflict fought between the Axis powers (Germany, Italy, and Japan) and the victorious Allied powers (United Kingdom and its colonies, France, the Soviet Union, and the United States).

84. **World Wildlife Fund:** a nongovernmental organization that promotes biodiversity, conservation, and limiting the environmental impact that humans have on the planet.

PEOPLE MENTIONED IN THE TEXT

1. **Aristotle (384–322 B.C.E.)** was a Greek philosopher. Together with his teacher, Plato, he is one of the key originators of Western philosophy. Most of Aristotle's extant works, such as *Nicomachean Ethics* and *Metaphysics*, are treatises written for educational purposes in his school, the Lyceum.

2. **Bashar al-Assad (b. 1965)** has been the president of Syria since 2000. The second-born son of Hafez al-Assad, he originally trained as a doctor of ophthalmology but was named heir to his president father after his older brother died unexpectedly in 1994.

3. **John Bolton (b. 1948)** is a neoconservative political commentator and diplomat, who served as the US ambassador to the United Nations from August 2005 until December 2006.

4. **Napoleon Bonaparte (1769–1821)** was among the youngest and most successful generals of revolutionary France in the 1790s. In 1804, he declared himself emperor of the French and, following a series of shattering victories, established French domination over much of continental Europe. He was defeated at the Battle of Waterloo in 1815 and exiled to St. Helena in the South Atlantic.

5. **Stephen Brooks** is an associate professor of government at Dartmouth College. He is known for his collaboration with William Wohlforth, and his book *Producing Security: Multinational Corporations, Globalization, and the Changing Calculus of Conflict.*

6. **George H. W. Bush (b. 1924)** was the 41st president of the United States, vice-president to Ronald Reagan, served as director of the Central Intelligence Agency, and was a diplomat.

7. **George W. Bush (b. 1946)** was the 43rd president of the United States. He served two terms, from 2001 to 2009.

8. **Jimmy Carter (b. 1924)** was the 39th president of the United States. He is best known for presiding over the Iranian Revolution.

9. **Lord Castlereagh** was an Irish and British statesman, and secretary of state for foreign affairs. He is best remembered for representing Britain at the Congress of Vienna in 1814–15.

10. **Bill Clinton (b. 1946)** was the 42nd president of the United States, in office from 1993 to 2001.

11. **Hillary Clinton (b. 1947)** is an American politician and diplomat. Secretary of state between 2009 and 2013, she became a candidate in the 2016 presidential elections.

12. **Dwight D. Eisenhower (1890–1969)** was the 34th president of the United States and commanding general of the Allied forces during World War II.

13. **William Y. Elliott (1896–1979)** was a prominent American historian, who served on the US National Security Council staff following World War II, and advised six American presidents. He was Henry Kissinger's mentor at Harvard.

14. **Gerald Ford (1913–2006)** was the 38th president of the United States. He was a member of the House of Representatives until 1973, when he was selected as President Richard Nixon's vice-president after a scandal forced the resignation of his predecessor, Spiro Agnew. He became president upon Nixon's resignation in August 1974.

15. **Francis Fukuyama (b. 1952)** is an American political scientist, political economist, and author.

16. **Adolf Hitler (1889–1945)** was leader of the Nazi Party and dictator of Germany 1933–1945. His expansionist policies provoked World War II.

17. **Samuel P. Huntington (1927–2008)** was a professor of international relations at Harvard University. His book, *The Clash of Civilizations and the Remaking of World Order* is widely considered the most influential post-Cold War analysis of international order.

18. **Wolfgang Ischinger (b. 1946)** is a German diplomat, who served as the German ambassador to the United States from 2001 to 2006.

19. **Robert Kagan (b. 1958)** is an American neoconservative political commentator, who has served as an advisor to Hillary Clinton, John Kerry, and John McCain.

20. **Immanuel Kant (1724–1804)** was a Prussian philosopher (what is now modern Germany), who was best known for his defense of the idea that all people were worthy of equal consideration and respect, based on the idea that one should act

| People Mentioned in the Text

as though one's actions were the universal law (the "categorical imperative").

21. **Paul Kennedy (b. 1945)** is a British-born professor of history at Yale University, who is known for his work on international relations. He is best known for his book *The Rise and Fall of the Great Powers* (1987).

22. **Robert Keohane (b. 1941)** is an American political science professor at Princeton. He is associated with neoliberal institutionalism—based on the notion that international institutions can encourage cooperation between states—and, notably, wrote *Power and Interdependence* with Joseph Nye.

23. **Fritz Kraemer (1908–2003)** was a German-born American military advisor, who convinced close friend Henry Kissinger to further his education.

24. **Niccolò Machiavelli (1469–1527)** was an Italian philosopher and diplomat, best known as the author of *The Prince*, in which he argued that the use of force and immoral behavior are sometimes necessary to retain power; this is justifiable because no means should be spared to achieve this end.

25. **John Mearsheimer (b. 1947)** is a professor of international relations at the University of Chicago. His 2001 work, *The Tragedy of Great Power Politics*, established him as a leading international relations theorist in the neorealist school of political thought. This text introduced the theory of offensive realism.

26. **Klemens Wenzel von Metternich (1773–1859)** was an Austrian prince, diplomat, and state chancellor between 1821 and 1848. He played a pivotal role in bringing about the Congress of Vienna, which established a new order in Europe.

27. **Hans Morgenthau (1904–80)** was a German political theorist who worked primarily in America. He has been described as the most prominent of the classical realists.

28. **Prophet Muhammad (c.e. 570–632)** was the founder of Islam. Starting in 610, he experienced a series of prophetic experiences that were later transcribed into the Islamic holy book, the Koran, which became the basis of Islamic doctrine and legislation (*shari'a*).

29. **Vali Nasr (b. 1960)** is an American political scientist who specializes in the

international relations of the Middle East. He is currently the dean of the School of Advanced International Studies at Johns Hopkins University.

30. **Richard Nixon (1913–94)** was the 37th president of the United States and the first American president to resign from office, having been embroiled in the Watergate scandal.

31. **Joseph Nye, Jr. (b. 1937)** is an American political science professor at Harvard. Together with Robert Keohane he wrote *Power and Interdependence* (1977), effectively founding neoliberal institutionalism.

32. **Barack Obama (b. 1961)** is the 44th president of the United States and was elected in 2008. He is the country's first black president.

33. **Lord Palmerston (1784–1865)** was prime minister of Britain from 1855 to 1858 and from 1859 to 1865.

34. **Leopold von Ranke (1795–1886)** was a German historian who founded a methodological approach aimed at developing historical narratives based on archival research.

35. **Nelson Rockefeller (1908–79)** was the 41st vice-president of the United States, the 49th governor of New York, a prominent American businessman, and a philanthropist; he hailed from the wealthy Rockefeller family.

36. **Theodore Roosevelt (1858–1919)** was the 26th president of the United States. He is best known for his association with the realist school of thought.

37. **Anne-Marie Slaughter (b. 1958)** is a professor of politics and international affairs at Princeton, a foreign-policy analyst, and currently the president of the New America Foundation.

38. **Benedict de Spinoza (1632–77)** was a Jewish Dutch philosopher in the rationalist tradition. His main works are *Tractatus Logico-Politicus* and *Ethics*.

39. **Joseph Stalin (1878–1953)** led the Soviet Union from 1924 to 1953.

40. **Thucydides (c. 460–395 B.C.E.)** was a Greek historian, best known for a chronicle of the 431–404 B.C.E. war between Athens and Sparta entitled *The History of the Peloponnesian War*. He is considered to be one of the first

proponents of "realpolitik," the idea that power and interests should take precedence over ideas and ethics in politics.

41. **James Traub (b. 1954)** is an American journalist who specializes in international affairs and writes for the *New York Times*.

42. **Stephen Walt (b. 1955)** is a professor of international relations at Harvard University and a leading international relations theorist from the neorealist school of political thought. He developed the theoretical concept known as "balance of threat."

43. **Woodrow Wilson (1856–1924)** was the 28th president of the United States of America, from 1913 to 1921. He is best known for his liberal idealist principles and his role in attempting to reconstruct Europe on democratic principles after World War I.

44. **William Wohlforth (b. 1959)** is an American professor of government at Dartmouth College. He is best known for his collaborations with Stephen Brooks, and his text *The Elusive Balance: Power and Perceptions during the Cold War* (1993).

45. **Paul Wolfowitz (b. 1943)** is a neoconservative scholar, a former president of the World Bank, and was a deputy secretary of defense during the George W. Bush administration. He played a pivotal role in bringing about the ill-fated Iraq War.

46. **Fareed Zakaria (b. 1964)** is an Indian American journalist, author, and neorealist scholar. He has been managing editor of *Foreign Affairs*, editor-at-large at *Time* and, notably, authored *The Post-American World*.

WORKS CITED

1. Arms Control Association. "Iran Nuclear Negotiations: Separating Myth from Reality." *Issue Briefs* 7, no. 2 (January 2015). Accessed November 4, 2015. https://www.armscontrol.org/issue-briefs/2015-01-23/Iran-Nuclear-Negotiations-Separating-Myth-from-Reality.

2. Brooks, Stephen G., and William C. Wohlforth. "Reshaping the World Order." *Foreign Affairs* (March/April 2009): 49-63. Accessed December 7, 2015. https://www.foreignaffairs.com/articles/2009-03-01/reshaping-world-order.

3. Centers for Disease Control and Prevention. "2014 Ebola Outbreak in West Africa–Case Counts." Accessed November 18, 2015. http://www.cdc.gov/vhf/ebola/outbreaks/2014-west-africa/case-counts.html.

4. Clinton, Hillary R. "Hillary Clinton Reviews Henry Kissinger's *World Order*." *Washington Post*, September 4, 2014. Accessed September 18, 2015. https://www.washingtonpost.com/opinions/hillary-clinton-reviews-henry-kissingers-world-order/2014/09/04/b280c654-31ea-11e4-8f02-03c644b2d7d0_story.html.

5. Dallek, Robert. *Nixon and Kissinger: Partners in Power*. London: HarperCollins, 2007.

6. Drezner, Daniel W. "The New New World Order." *Foreign Affairs* (March/April 2007): 34–46. Accessed December 7, 2015. https://www.foreignaffairs.com/articles/2007-03-01/new-new-world-order.

7. *Economist*. "A Bit of a Mess," September 6, 2014. Accessed September 10, 2015. http://www.economist.com/news/books-and-arts/21615478-geopolitics-henry-kissinger-grand-and-gloomy-bit-mess.

8. Fukuyama, Francis. *The End of History and the Last Man*. New York: Free Press, 2006.

9. Hitchens, Christopher. *The Trial of Henry Kissinger*. London: Verso, 2001.

10. Huntington, Samuel. "The Clash of Civilizations?" *Foreign Affairs* (Summer 1993): 22–49. Accessed December 7, 2015. https://www.foreignaffairs.com/articles/united-states/1993-06-01/clash-civilizations.

11. _____. *The Clash of Civilizations and the Remaking of World Order*. New York:

Simon and Schuster, 1996.

12. Ischinger, Wolfgang. "The World According to Kissinger: How to Defend Global Order." *Foreign Affairs* (March/April 2015). Accessed October 1, 2015. https:// www.foreignaffairs.com/reviews/2015-03-01/world-according-kissinger.

13. Kennedy, Paul. *The Parliament of Man: The Past, Present, and Future of the United Nations.* New York: Random House, 2006.

14. Kissinger, Henry. "A Path Out of the Middle East Collapse." *Wall Street Journal*, October 16, 2015. Accessed October 22, 2015. http://www.wsj.com/articles/a-path-out-of-the-middle-east-collapse-1445037513.

15. ———. *A World Restored: Metternich, Castlereagh and the Problems of Peace, 1812–22.* New York: Weidenfeld and Nicolson, 1957.

16. ———. *American Foreign Policy: Three Essays.* New York: W. W. Norton, 1969.

17. ———. *Diplomacy.* New York: Simon and Schuster, 1994.

18. ———. *Nuclear Weapons and Foreign Policy.* New York: Harper & Brothers, 1957.

19. ———. *On China.* New York: Penguin, 2011.

20. ———. *The Necessity for Choice: Prospects of American Foreign Policy.* New York: Doubleday, 1961.

21. ———. *The Troubled Partnership: A Reappraisal of the Atlantic Alliance.* New York: McGraw-Hill, 1965.

22. ———. *White House Years.* Boston: Little, Brown, 1979.

23. ———. *World Order.* New York: Penguin, 2015.

24. ———. *Years of Renewal.* New York: Simon and Schuster, 1999.

25. ———. *Years of Upheaval.* Boston: Little, Brown, 1982.

26. Marans, Daniel. "Henry Kissinger Just Turned 92. Here's Why He's Careful About Where He Travels." *Huffington Post*, May 27, 2015. Accessed October 9, 2015. http://www.huffingtonpost.com/2015/05/27/henry-kissinger-human-rights_

n_7454172.html.

27. Mearsheimer, John J. *The Tragedy of Great Power Politics*. New York: W. W. Norton, 2001.

28. ———. "Why The Ukraine Crisis is the West's Fault." *Foreign Affairs* (September/ October 2014). Accessed October 16, 2015. http://www.foreignaffairs.com/ articles/141769/john-j-mearsheimer/why-the-ukraine-crisis-is-the-wests-fault.

29. Micklethwait, John. "As the World Turns: Henry Kissinger's 'World Order.'" *New York Times*, September 11, 2014. Accessed December 7, 2015. http://www. nytimes.com/2014/09/14/books/review/henry-kissingers-world-order.html?_r=0.

30. Mitter, Rana. "'World Order' by Henry Kissinger–review." *Guardian*, October 1, 2014. Accessed October 15, 2015. http://www.theguardian.com/books/2014/oct/01/world-order-by-henry-kissinger-review-account.

31. Morgenthau, Hans. *Politics Among Nations: The Struggle for Power and Peace*. New York: Knopf, 1948.

32. ———. "Review: *Nuclear Weapons and Foreign Policy* by Henry Kissinger." *American Political Science Review* 52, no. 3 (September 1958): 842–4.

33. Nye, Jr., Joseph S. "What New World Order?" *Foreign Affairs* (Spring 1992): 83–96. Accessed December 7, 2015. https://www.foreignaffairs.com/articles/1992-03-01/what-new-world-order.

34. Slaughter, Anne-Marie. "A No-Fly Zone for Syria." *Project Syndicate*, August 25, 2015. Accessed October 22, 2015. http://www.project-syndicate.org/commentary/no-fly-zone-syria-by-anne-marie-slaughter-2015-08.

35. ———. "How to Fix America's Foreign Policy." *New Republic*, November 19, 2014. Accessed September 18, 2015. http://www.newrepublic.com/article/120030/ world-order-review-what-obama-should-learn-kissingers-book.

36. ———. "The Real New World Order." *Foreign Affairs* (September/October 1997): 183–97. Accessed December 7, 2015. https://www.foreignaffairs.com/articles/1997-09-01/real-new-world-order.

37. Traub, James. "Book Review: *World Order* by Henry Kissinger." *Wall Street Journal*, September 5, 2014. Accessed September 18, 2015. http://www.wsj.com/articles/book-review-world-order-by-henry-kissinger-1409952751.

38. Zakaria, Fareed. "Ask Fareed Zakaria Anything: Stay Out of Syria." *The Dish*, June 7, 2013. Accessed October 16, 2015. http://dish.andrewsullivan.com/2013/06/07/ask-fareed-zakaria-anything-stay-out-of-syria/.

原书作者简介

亨利·基辛格1923年生于德国南部，1938年与其犹太家族一道逃离纳粹统治，前往美国。他一开始投身于学术界，但很快转向了政界。作为美国总统尼克松和福特的国家安全顾问（1969—1975）和国务卿（1973—1977），基辛格在美国历史上的这段重要时期负责美国的外交政策。他于1973年促成了美国从越南撤兵，因此获得了诺贝尔和平奖。1977年离开公职后，基辛格一直在外交政策方面建言献策，从未间断。

本书作者简介

布莱恩·R.吉布森博士获伦敦政治经济学院国际史博士学位，曾任伦敦政治经济学院外交与战略中心博士后研究员，伦敦政治经济学院国际史学院和东英吉利大学政治、社会和国际学学院中东政治学讲师。

他现供职于约翰斯·霍普金斯大学，是《售罄？美国外交政策、伊拉克、库尔德人和冷战》（帕尔格雷夫·麦克米兰出版公司，2015）一书的作者。

世界名著中的批判性思维

《世界思想宝库钥匙丛书》致力于深入浅出地阐释全世界著名思想家的观点，不论是谁、在何处都能了解到，从而推进批判性思维发展。

《世界思想宝库钥匙丛书》与世界顶尖大学的一流学者合作，为一系列学科中最有影响的著作推出新的分析文本，介绍其观点和影响。在这一不断扩展的系列中，每种选入的著作都代表了历经时间考验的思想典范。通过为这些著作提供必要背景、揭示原作者的学术渊源以及说明这些著作所产生的影响，本系列图书希望让读者以新视角看待这些划时代的经典之作。读者应学会思考、运用并挑战这些著作中的观点，而不是简单接受它们。

ABOUT THE AUTHOR OF THE ORIGINAL WORK

Born in southern Germany in 1923, **Henry Kissinger** fled with his Jewish family to the United States to escape the Nazis in 1938. He began his career in academia, but soon turned to politics. As national security advisor to US presidents Nixon and Ford (1969–75), and as secretary of state (1973–77), Kissinger was responsible for American foreign policy during a critical period in the country's history. He won the Nobel Peace Prize for helping bring about the American withdrawal from Vietnam in 1973. Since leaving public office in 1977, Kissinger has continued to advise on foreign policy.

ABOUT THE AUTHOR OF THE ANALYSIS

Dr Bryan R. Gibson holds a PhD in International History from the London School of Economics (LSE) and was a post-doctoral research fellow at the LSE's Centre for Diplomacy and Strategy and an instructor on Middle Eastern politics at both the LSE's Department of International History and the University of East Anglia's Department of Political, Social and International Studies (PSI).

He is currently on the faculty of Johns Hopkins University and is the author of *Sold Out? US Foreign Policy, Iraq, the Kurds and the Cold War* (Palgrave Macmillan, 2015).

ABOUT MACAT
GREAT WORKS FOR CRITICAL THINKING

Macat is focused on making the ideas of the world's great thinkers accessible and comprehensible to everybody, everywhere, in ways that promote the development of enhanced critical thinking skills.

It works with leading academics from the world's top universities to produce new analyses that focus on the ideas and the impact of the most influential works ever written across a wide variety of academic disciplines. Each of the works that sit at the heart of its growing library is an enduring example of great thinking. But by setting them in context — and looking at the influences that shaped their authors, as well as the responses they provoked — Macat encourages readers to look at these classics and game-changers with fresh eyes. Readers learn to think, engage and challenge their ideas, rather than simply accepting them.

批判性思维与《世界秩序》

首要批判性思维技巧：阐释
次要批判性思维技巧：理性化思维

　　亨利·基辛格是 20 世纪最有名的政治家之一，在他漫长的政治生涯中对世界舞台产生了一定影响，他的 2014 年著作《世界秩序：反思国家特征和历史进程》即反映了他长期政治生涯中形成的思想观点，也是对国际政治理论的一大贡献。基辛格最初从事学术研究，并接受大学教职，后于 1973 年被美国总统理查德·尼克松任命为美国国务卿。正是在这一职位上，他获颁诺贝尔和平奖，而反越战的抗议者则指控他在越南犯下战争罪行。虽然基辛格是一位具有争议性的人物，但大家一致公认，基辛格在政治和国际关系领域展示了无与伦比的实践和理论才能。《世界秩序》就是他在这些领域中毕生研究的结晶。

　　《世界秩序》致力于界定当今全球政治中的各种世界观，展示了大师级的阐释技巧。世界各国对于"秩序"是如何构想的？通过阐明这一点，基辛格凸显了全球政治的各种挑战，让人们能够采取更清晰的视角去尝试弥合分歧。基辛格的历史功过如何评说，也许仍是一个见仁见智的问题，但他的《世界秩序》是一部使人欲罢不能、茅塞顿开的作品，其出色的阐释技巧是毋庸置疑的。

CRITICAL THINKING AND *WORLD ORDER*

- Primary critical thinking skill: INTERPRETATION
- Secondary critical thinking skill: REASONING

Henry Kissinger's 2014 book *World Order: Reflections on the Character of Nations and the Course of History* not only offers a summary of thinking developed throughout a long and highly influential career—it is also an intervention in international relations theory by one of the most famous statesmen of the twentieth century. Kissinger initially trained as a university professor before becoming Secretary of State to President Richard Nixon in 1973—a position in which he both won the Nobel Peace Prize and was accused of war crimes by protesters against American military actions in Vietnam. While a controversial figure, Kissinger is widely agreed to have a unique level of practical and theoretical expertise in politics and international relations—and *World Order* is the culmination of a lifetime's experience of work in those fields.

The product of a master of the critical thinking skill of interpretation, *World Order* takes on the challenge of defining the worldviews at play in global politics today. Clarifying precisely what is meant by the different notions of "order" imagined by nations across the world, as Kissinger does, highlights the challenges of world politics, and sharpens the focus on efforts to make surmounting these divisions possible. While Kissinger's own reputation will likely remain equivocal, there is no doubting the interpretative skills he displays in this engaging and illuminating text.

《世界思想宝库钥匙丛书》简介

《世界思想宝库钥匙丛书》致力于为一系列在各领域产生重大影响的人文社科类经典著作提供独特的学术探讨。每一本读物都不仅仅是原经典著作的内容摘要，而是介绍并深入研究原经典著作的学术渊源、主要观点和历史影响。这一丛书的目的是提供一套学习资料，以促进读者掌握批判性思维，从而更全面、深刻地去理解重要思想。

每一本读物分为3个部分：学术渊源、学术思想和学术影响，每个部分下有4个小节。这些章节旨在从各个方面研究原经典著作及其反响。

由于独特的体例，每一本读物不但易于阅读，而且另有一项优点：所有读物的编排体例相同，读者在进行某个知识层面的调查或研究时可交叉参阅多本该丛书中的相关读物，从而开启跨领域研究的路径。

为了方便阅读，每本读物最后还列出了术语表和人名表（在书中则以星号 * 标记），此外还有参考文献。

《世界思想宝库钥匙丛书》与剑桥大学合作，理清了批判性思维的要点，即如何通过6种技能来进行有效思考。其中3种技能让我们能够理解问题，另3种技能让我们有能力解决问题。这6种技能合称为"批判性思维 PACIER 模式"，它们是：

分析：了解如何建立一个观点；
评估：研究一个观点的优点和缺点；
阐释：对意义所产生的问题加以理解；
创造性思维：提出新的见解，发现新的联系；
解决问题：提出切实有效的解决办法；
理性化思维：创建有说服力的观点。

THE MACAT LIBRARY

The Macat Library is a series of unique academic explorations of seminal works in the humanities and social sciences — books and papers that have had a significant and widely recognised impact on their disciplines. It has been created to serve as much more than just a summary of what lies between the covers of a great book. It illuminates and explores the influences on, ideas of, and impact of that book. Our goal is to offer a learning resource that encourages critical thinking and fosters a better, deeper understanding of important ideas.

Each publication is divided into three Sections: Influences, Ideas, and Impact. Each Section has four Modules. These explore every important facet of the work, and the responses to it.

This Section-Module structure makes a Macat Library book easy to use, but it has another important feature. Because each Macat book is written to the same format, it is possible (and encouraged!) to cross-reference multiple Macat books along the same lines of inquiry or research. This allows the reader to open up interesting interdisciplinary pathways.

To further aid your reading, lists of glossary terms and people mentioned are included at the end of this book (these are indicated by an asterisk [*] throughout) — as well as a list of works cited.

Macat has worked with the University of Cambridge to identify the elements of critical thinking and understand the ways in which six different skills combine to enable effective thinking.

Three allow us to fully understand a problem; three more give us the tools to solve it. Together, these six skills make up the PACIER model of critical thinking. They are:

ANALYSIS — understanding how an argument is built
EVALUATION — exploring the strengths and weaknesses of an argument
INTERPRETATION — understanding issues of meaning
CREATIVE THINKING — coming up with new ideas and fresh connections
PROBLEM-SOLVING — producing strong solutions
REASONING — creating strong arguments

"《世界思想宝库钥匙丛书》提供了独一无二的跨学科学习和研究工具。它介绍那些革新了各自学科研究的经典著作，还邀请全世界一流专家和教育机构进行严谨的分析，为每位读者打开世界顶级教育的大门。"

——安德烈亚斯·施莱歇尔，
经济合作与发展组织教育与技能司司长

"《世界思想宝库钥匙丛书》直面大学教育的巨大挑战……他们组建了一支精干而活跃的学者队伍，来推出在研究广度上颇具新意的教学材料。"

——布罗尔斯教授、勋爵，剑桥大学前校长

"《世界思想宝库钥匙丛书》的愿景令人赞叹。它通过分析和阐释那些曾深刻影响人类思想以及社会、经济发展的经典文本，提供了新的学习方法。它推动批判性思维，这对于任何社会和经济体来说都是至关重要的。这就是未来的学习方法。"

——查尔斯·克拉克阁下，英国前教育大臣

"对于那些影响了各自领域的著作，《世界思想宝库钥匙丛书》能让人们立即了解到围绕那些著作展开的评论性言论，这让该系列图书成为在这些领域从事研究的师生们不可或缺的资源。"

——威廉·特朗佐教授，加利福尼亚大学圣地亚哥分校

"Macat offers an amazing first-of-its-kind tool for interdisciplinary learning and research. Its focus on works that transformed their disciplines and its rigorous approach, drawing on the world's leading experts and educational institutions, opens up a world-class education to anyone."

―― Andreas Schleicher, Director for Education and Skills, Organisation for Economic Co-operation and Development

"Macat is taking on some of the major challenges in university education... They have drawn together a strong team of active academics who are producing teaching materials that are novel in the breadth of their approach."

―― Prof Lord Broers, former Vice-Chancellor of the University of Cambridge

"The Macat vision is exceptionally exciting. It focuses upon new modes of learning which analyse and explain seminal texts which have profoundly influenced world thinking and so social and economic development. It promotes the kind of critical thinking which is essential for any society and economy. This is the learning of the future."

―― Rt Hon Charles Clarke, former UK Secretary of State for Education

"The Macat analyses provide immediate access to the critical conversation surrounding the books that have shaped their respective discipline, which will make them an invaluable resource to all of those, students and teachers, working in the field."

―― Prof William Tronzo, University of California at San Diego

The Macat Library
世界思想宝库钥匙丛书

TITLE	中文书名	类别
An Analysis of Arjun Appadurai's *Modernity at Large: Cultural Dimensions of Globalization*	解析阿尔君·阿帕杜莱《消失的现代性：全球化的文化维度》	人类学
An Analysis of Claude Lévi-Strauss's *Structural Anthropology*	解析克劳德·列维-斯特劳斯《结构人类学》	人类学
An Analysis of Marcel Mauss's *The Gift*	解析马塞尔·莫斯《礼物》	人类学
An Analysis of Jared M. Diamond's *Guns, Germs, and Steel: The Fate of Human Societies*	解析贾雷德·M. 戴蒙德《枪炮、病菌与钢铁：人类社会的命运》	人类学
An Analysis of Clifford Geertz's *The Interpretation of Cultures*	解析克利福德·格尔茨《文化的解释》	人类学
An Analysis of Philippe Ariès's *Centuries of Childhood: A Social History of Family Life*	解析菲力浦·阿利埃斯《儿童的世纪：旧制度下的儿童和家庭生活》	人类学
An Analysis of W. Chan Kim & Renée Mauborgne's *Blue Ocean Strategy*	解析金伟灿/勒妮·莫博涅《蓝海战略》	商业
An Analysis of John P. Kotter's *Leading Change*	解析约翰·P. 科特《领导变革》	商业
An Analysis of Michael E. Porter's *Competitive Strategy: Techniques for Analyzing Industries and Competitors*	解析迈克尔·E. 波特《竞争战略：分析产业和竞争对手的技术》	商业
An Analysis of Jean Lave & Etienne Wenger's *Situated Learning: Legitimate Peripheral Participation*	解析琼·莱夫/艾蒂纳·温格《情境学习：合法的边缘性参与》	商业
An Analysis of Douglas McGregor's *The Human Side of Enterprise*	解析道格拉斯·麦格雷戈《企业的人性面》	商业
An Analysis of Milton Friedman's *Capitalism and Freedom*	解析米尔顿·弗里德曼《资本主义与自由》	商业
An Analysis of Ludwig von Mises's *The Theory of Money and Credit*	解析路德维希·冯·米塞斯《货币和信用理论》	经济学
An Analysis of Adam Smith's *The Wealth of Nations*	解析亚当·斯密《国富论》	经济学
An Analysis of Thomas Piketty's *Capital in the Twenty-First Century*	解析托马斯·皮凯蒂《21世纪资本论》	经济学
An Analysis of Nassim Nicholas Taleb's *The Black Swan: The Impact of the Highly Improbable*	解析纳西姆·尼古拉斯·塔勒布《黑天鹅：如何应对不可预知的未来》	经济学
An Analysis of Ha-Joon Chang's *Kicking Away the Ladder*	解析张夏准《富国陷阱：发达国家为何踢开梯子》	经济学
An Analysis of Thomas Robert Malthus's *An Essay on the Principle of Population*	解析托马斯·罗伯特·马尔萨斯《人口论》	经济学

An Analysis of John Maynard Keynes's *The General Theory of Employment, Interest and Money*	解析约翰·梅纳德·凯恩斯《就业、利息和货币通论》	经济学
An Analysis of Milton Friedman's *The Role of Monetary Policy*	解析米尔顿·弗里德曼《货币政策的作用》	经济学
An Analysis of Burton G. Malkiel's *A Random Walk Down Wall Street*	解析伯顿·G.马尔基尔《漫步华尔街》	经济学
An Analysis of Friedrich A. Hayek's *The Road to Serfdom*	解析弗里德里希·A.哈耶克《通往奴役之路》	经济学
An Analysis of Charles P. Kindleberger's *Manias, Panics, and Crashes: A History of Financial Crises*	解析查尔斯·P.金德尔伯格《疯狂、惊恐和崩溃：金融危机史》	经济学
An Analysis of Amartya Sen's *Development as Freedom*	解析阿马蒂亚·森《以自由看待发展》	经济学
An Analysis of Rachel Carson's *Silent Spring*	解析蕾切尔·卡森《寂静的春天》	地理学
An Analysis of Charles Darwin's *On the Origin of Species: by Means of Natural Selection, or The Preservation of Favoured Races in the Struggle for Life*	解析查尔斯·达尔文《物种起源》	地理学
An Analysis of World Commission on Environment and Development's *The Brundtland Report: Our Common Future*	解析世界环境与发展委员会《布伦特兰报告：我们共同的未来》	地理学
An Analysis of James E. Lovelock's *Gaia: A New Look at Life on Earth*	解析詹姆斯·E.拉伍洛克《盖娅：地球生命的新视野》	地理学
An Analysis of Paul Kennedy's *The Rise and Fall of the Great Powers: Economic Change and Military Conflict from 1500–2000*	解析保罗·肯尼迪《大国的兴衰：1500—2000年的经济变革与军事冲突》	历史
An Analysis of Janet L. Abu-Lughod's *Before European Hegemony: The World System A. D. 1250–1350*	解析珍妮特·L.阿布-卢格霍德《欧洲霸权之前：1250—1350年的世界体系》	历史
An Analysis of Alfred W. Crosby's *The Columbian Exchange: Biological and Cultural Consequences of 1492*	解析艾尔弗雷德·W.克罗斯比《哥伦布大交换：1492年以后的生物影响和文化冲击》	历史
An Analysis of Tony Judt's *Postwar: A History of Europe since 1945*	解析托尼·朱特《战后欧洲史》	历史
An Analysis of Richard J. Evans's *In Defence of History*	解析理查德·J.艾文斯《捍卫历史》	历史
An Analysis of Eric Hobsbawm's *The Age of Revolution: Europe 1789–1848*	解析艾瑞克·霍布斯鲍姆《革命的年代：欧洲1789—1848年》	历史

An Analysis of Roland Barthes's *Mythologies*	解析罗兰·巴特《神话学》	文学与批判理论
An Analysis of Simone de Beauvoir's *The Second Sex*	解析西蒙娜·德·波伏娃《第二性》	文学与批判理论
An Analysis of Edward W. Said's *Orientalism*	解析爱德华·W. 萨义德《东方主义》	文学与批判理论
An Analysis of Virginia Woolf's *A Room of One's Own*	解析弗吉尼亚·伍尔芙《一间自己的房间》	文学与批判理论
An Analysis of Judith Butler's *Gender Trouble*	解析朱迪斯·巴特勒《性别麻烦》	文学与批判理论
An Analysis of Ferdinand de Saussure's *Course in General Linguistics*	解析费尔迪南·德·索绪尔《普通语言学教程》	文学与批判理论
An Analysis of Susan Sontag's *On Photography*	解析苏珊·桑塔格《论摄影》	文学与批判理论
An Analysis of Walter Benjamin's *The Work of Art in the Age of Mechanical Reproduction*	解析瓦尔特·本雅明《机械复制时代的艺术作品》	文学与批判理论
An Analysis of W. E. B. Du Bois's *The Souls of Black Folk*	解析W.E.B. 杜波依斯《黑人的灵魂》	文学与批判理论
An Analysis of Plato's *The Republic*	解析柏拉图《理想国》	哲学
An Analysis of Plato's *Symposium*	解析柏拉图《会饮篇》	哲学
An Analysis of Aristotle's *Metaphysics*	解析亚里士多德《形而上学》	哲学
An Analysis of Aristotle's *Nicomachean Ethics*	解析亚里士多德《尼各马可伦理学》	哲学
An Analysis of Immanuel Kant's *Critique of Pure Reason*	解析伊曼努尔·康德《纯粹理性批判》	哲学
An Analysis of Ludwig Wittgenstein's *Philosophical Investigations*	解析路德维希·维特根斯坦《哲学研究》	哲学
An Analysis of G. W. F. Hegel's *Phenomenology of Spirit*	解析G.W.F. 黑格尔《精神现象学》	哲学
An Analysis of Baruch Spinoza's *Ethics*	解析巴鲁赫·斯宾诺莎《伦理学》	哲学
An Analysis of Hannah Arendt's *The Human Condition*	解析汉娜·阿伦特《人的境况》	哲学
An Analysis of G. E. M. Anscombe's *Modern Moral Philosophy*	解析G.E.M. 安斯康姆《现代道德哲学》	哲学
An Analysis of David Hume's *An Enquiry Concerning Human Understanding*	解析大卫·休谟《人类理解研究》	哲学

An Analysis of Søren Kierkegaard's *Fear and Trembling*	解析索伦·克尔凯郭尔《恐惧与战栗》	哲学
An Analysis of René Descartes's *Meditations on First Philosophy*	解析勒内·笛卡尔《第一哲学沉思录》	哲学
An Analysis of Friedrich Nietzsche's *On the Genealogy of Morality*	解析弗里德里希·尼采《论道德的谱系》	哲学
An Analysis of Gilbert Ryle's *The Concept of Mind*	解析吉尔伯特·赖尔《心的概念》	哲学
An Analysis of Thomas Kuhn's *The Structure of Scientific Revolutions*	解析托马斯·库恩《科学革命的结构》	哲学
An Analysis of John Stuart Mill's *Utilitarianism*	解析约翰·斯图亚特·穆勒《功利主义》	哲学
An Analysis of Aristotle's *Politics*	解析亚里士多德《政治学》	政治学
An Analysis of Niccolò Machiavelli's *The Prince*	解析尼科洛·马基雅维利《君主论》	政治学
An Analysis of Karl Marx's *Capital*	解析卡尔·马克思《资本论》	政治学
An Analysis of Benedict Anderson's *Imagined Communities*	解析本尼迪克特·安德森《想象的共同体》	政治学
An Analysis of Samuel P. Huntington's *The Clash of Civilizations and the Remaking of World Order*	解析塞缪尔·P.亨廷顿《文明的冲突与世界秩序的重建》	政治学
An Analysis of Alexis de Tocqueville's *Democracy in America*	解析阿列克西·德·托克维尔《论美国的民主》	政治学
An Analysis of John A. Hobson's *Imperialism: A Study*	解析约翰·A.霍布森《帝国主义》	政治学
An Analysis of Thomas Paine's *Common Sense*	解析托马斯·潘恩《常识》	政治学
An Analysis of John Rawls's *A Theory of Justice*	解析约翰·罗尔斯《正义论》	政治学
An Analysis of Francis Fukuyama's *The End of History and the Last Man*	解析弗朗西斯·福山《历史的终结与最后的人》	政治学
An Analysis of John Locke's *Two Treatises of Government*	解析约翰·洛克《政府论》	政治学
An Analysis of Sun Tzu's *The Art of War*	解析孙武《孙子兵法》	政治学
An Analysis of Henry Kissinger's *World Order: Reflections on the Character of Nations and the Course of History*	解析亨利·基辛格《世界秩序》	政治学
An Analysis of Jean-Jacques Rousseau's *The Social Contract*	解析让-雅克·卢梭《社会契约论》	政治学

An Analysis of Odd Arne Westad's *The Global Cold War: Third World Interventions and the Making of Our Times*	解析文安立《全球冷战：美苏对第三世界的干涉与当代世界的形成》	政治学
An Analysis of Sigmund Freud's *The Interpretation of Dreams*	解析西格蒙德·弗洛伊德《梦的解析》	心理学
An Analysis of William James' *The Principles of Psychology*	解析威廉·詹姆斯《心理学原理》	心理学
An Analysis of Philip Zimbardo's *The Lucifer Effect*	解析菲利普·津巴多《路西法效应》	心理学
An Analysis of Leon Festinger's *A Theory of Cognitive Dissonance*	解析利昂·费斯汀格《认知失调论》	心理学
An Analysis of Richard H. Thaler & Cass R. Sunstein's *Nudge: Improving Decisions about Health, Wealth, and Happiness*	解析理查德·H. 泰勒/卡斯·R. 桑斯坦《助推：如何做出有关健康、财富和幸福的更优决策》	心理学
An Analysis of Gordon Allport's *The Nature of Prejudice*	解析高尔登·奥尔波特《偏见的本质》	心理学
An Analysis of Steven Pinker's *The Better Angels of Our Nature: Why Violence Has Declined*	解析斯蒂芬·平克《人性中的善良天使：暴力为什么会减少》	心理学
An Analysis of Stanley Milgram's *Obedience to Authority*	解析斯坦利·米尔格拉姆《对权威的服从》	心理学
An Analysis of Betty Friedan's *The Feminine Mystique*	解析贝蒂·弗里丹《女性的奥秘》	心理学
An Analysis of David Riesman's *The Lonely Crowd: A Study of the Changing American Character*	解析大卫·理斯曼《孤独的人群：美国人社会性格演变之研究》	社会学
An Analysis of Franz Boas's *Race, Language and Culture*	解析弗朗兹·博厄斯《种族、语言与文化》	社会学
An Analysis of Pierre Bourdieu's *Outline of a Theory of Practice*	解析皮埃尔·布尔迪厄《实践理论大纲》	社会学
An Analysis of Max Weber's *The Protestant Ethic and the Spirit of Capitalism*	解析马克斯·韦伯《新教伦理与资本主义精神》	社会学
An Analysis of Jane Jacobs's *The Death and Life of Great American Cities*	解析简·雅各布斯《美国大城市的死与生》	社会学
An Analysis of C. Wright Mills's *The Sociological Imagination*	解析 C. 赖特·米尔斯《社会学的想象力》	社会学
An Analysis of Robert E. Lucas Jr.'s *Why Doesn't Capital Flow from Rich to Poor Countries?*	解析小罗伯特·E. 卢卡斯《为何资本不从富国流向穷国？》	社会学

An Analysis of Émile Durkheim's *On Suicide*	解析埃米尔·迪尔凯姆《自杀论》	社会学
An Analysis of Eric Hoffer's *The True Believer: Thoughts on the Nature of Mass Movements*	解析埃里克·霍弗《狂热分子：群众运动圣经》	社会学
An Analysis of Jared M. Diamond's *Collapse: How Societies Choose to Fail or Survive*	解析贾雷德·M.戴蒙德《大崩溃：社会如何选择兴亡》	社会学
An Analysis of Michel Foucault's *The History of Sexuality Vol. 1: The Will to Knowledge*	解析米歇尔·福柯《性史（第一卷）：求知意志》	社会学
An Analysis of Michel Foucault's *Discipline and Punish*	解析米歇尔·福柯《规训与惩罚》	社会学
An Analysis of Richard Dawkins's *The Selfish Gene*	解析理查德·道金斯《自私的基因》	社会学
An Analysis of Antonio Gramsci's *Prison Notebooks*	解析安东尼奥·葛兰西《狱中札记》	社会学
An Analysis of Augustine's *Confessions*	解析奥古斯丁《忏悔录》	神学
An Analysis of C. S. Lewis's *The Abolition of Man*	解析C. S.路易斯《人之废》	神学

图书在版编目（CIP）数据

解析亨利·基辛格《世界秩序》: 汉、英 / 布莱恩·R.吉布森（Bryan R. Gibson）著；于金权译. —上海：上海外语教育出版社, 2020
（世界思想宝库钥匙丛书）
ISBN 978-7-5446-6580-3

Ⅰ.①解… Ⅱ.①布…②于… Ⅲ.①国际政治－研究－汉、英 Ⅳ.①D5

中国版本图书馆CIP数据核字（2020）第217202号

This Chinese-English bilingual edition of *An Analysis of Henry Kissinger's* World Order: Reflections on the Character of Nations and the Course of History is published by arrangement with Macat International Limited.
Licensed for sale throughout the world.

本书汉英双语版由Macat国际有限公司授权上海外语教育出版社有限公司出版。
供在全世界范围内发行、销售。

图字：09－2018－549

出版发行：**上海外语教育出版社**
（上海外国语大学内） 邮编：200083
电　　话：021-65425300（总机）
电子邮箱：bookinfo@sflep.com.cn
网　　址：http://www.sflep.com
责任编辑：叶　青

印　　刷：上海信老印刷厂
开　　本：890×1240　1/32　印张 6　字数 124千字
版　　次：2021年7月第1版　2021年7月第1次印刷
书　　号：ISBN 978-7-5446-6580-3
定　　价：**30.00**元

本版图书如有印装质量问题，可向本社调换
质量服务热线：4008-213-263　电子邮箱：editorial@sflep.com